Contents

1.	Basic Concepts	1
2.	Accounting Changes and Errors	5
3A.	Inventory	6
3B.	Construction Accounting	9
4.	Operational Assets	10
5.	Monetary Current Assets and Liabilities	12
6A.	Time Value, Notes and Bonds	16
6B.	Debt Restructure	18
6C.	Pensions	19
6D.	Leases	21
7.	Deferred Taxes	24
8A.	Stockholders' Equity	25
8B.	Earnings Per Share	28
9.	Investments	29
10A.	Fake Cash Method	31
10B.	Statement of Cash Flows	32
11.	Consolidated Financial Statements	34
12.	Foreign Currency Transactions & Derivatives	36
13A.	Public Company Reporting	39
13B.	Partnership Accounting	40
13C.	Foreign Currency Translation	42
14.	Governmental Accounting	43
15.	Not-for-Profit Accounting	49

- FINANCIAL ACCOUNTING IS GOVERNED BY GAAP. THE SEC SETS GAAP & OVERSEES ITS PROPER USE. THE SEC HAS DELEGATED MOST OF THE TASK OF SETTING GAAP TO FASB WHICH IS FOR <u>PRIVATE SECTOR</u>. FOR PUBLIC SECTOR

- BOTH NOT-FOR-PROFIT & FOR PROFIT (PRIVATE SECTOR) RECORD GAAP IN THE ASC (ACCOUNTING STD.S CODIFICATION).

- FOR PUBLIC COMPANIES, SEC REQ. ADDITIONAL GAAPs WHICH ARE RECORDED IN ASC, CFR & SEC STAFF GUIDANCE.

- FOR STATE & LOCAL GOVTS., SEC DESIGNATES GASB TO DEVELOP GAAP WHICH IS RECORDED IN GASB CODIFICATION.

1. Basic Concepts

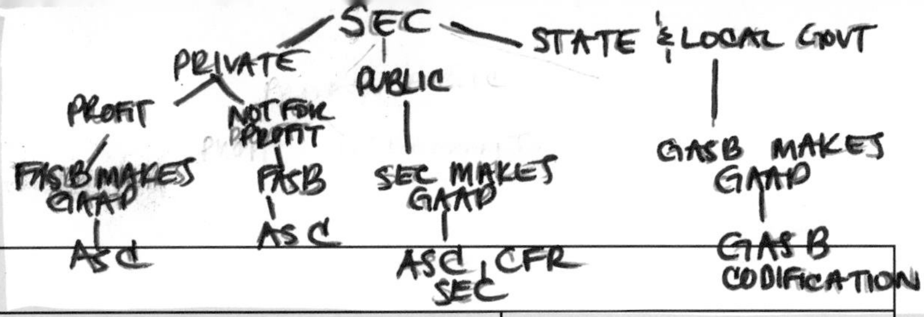

(handwritten diagram at top:)
SEC — STATE & LOCAL GOVT
PRIVATE / PUBLIC
PROFIT — NOT FOR PROFIT
FASB MAKES GAAP — FASB — SEC MAKES GAAP — GASB MAKES GAAP
ASC — ASC — ASC, CFR SEC — GASB CODIFICATION

For the private sector		For state and local governments
SEC designates	SEC issues	SEC designates
FASB to develop GAAP. FIN. ACCT. STD. BOARD	additional GAAP for public companies.	GASB to develop GAAP.

GAAP for for-profits are recorded in	GAAP for not-for-profits are recorded in	GAAP for public companies are recorded in	GAAP for state and local governments are recorded in
ASC.	ASC.	ASC, CFR, SEC staff guidance.	GASB Codification.

- All chapters deal with private sector for-profit accounting, shown in the first column above, unless stated otherwise.
- Since a college or hospital could be any of the above—private for-profit, private not-for-profit, public, or state/local government—the exam question will specify.

GAAP The body of accounting rules that is recognized as authoritative by SEC and AICPA. It includes the ASC, GASB codification, and the SEC rules and regulations found in the Code of Federal Regulations (CFR).

Accounting Standards Codification (ASC) The source document for all private-sector GAAP, except that which is published by the SEC. There is no hierarchy within ASC; it all carries an equal level of authority. As a service to users, the ASC includes some SEC rules, but the rule as written by the SEC is authoritative for public companies.

- The following is not GAAP: Statements of Financial Accounting Concepts, IFRS, widely recognized industry practices, AICPA Issues Papers, pronouncements of professional associations and regulatory agencies.

Statements of Financial Accounting Concepts Informs GAAP concepts without the force of GAAP. *(handwritten: (OBJECTIVES FOR THE PUBLIC, SET BY FASB.))*

Objective of reporting	• To provide information useful to existing and potential investors, lenders, and creditors.
Scope of reporting	• Information benefits must exceed costs of providing information, else not reported. • Information must be material in that omission could influence a user's decision, else not reported.

Qualitative characteristics of reporting	**Fundamental characteristics**
	 • Relevance
	   ○ Predictive value
	   ○ Confirmatory value
	 • Faithful representation
	   ○ Complete
	   ○ Neutral
	   ○ Free from error
	
	 Enhancing characteristics Enhances both relevance and faithful representation.
	 • **Comparability** One company to another.
	 • Verifiability
	 • **Timeliness** Downside of reporting too often is less faithful representation.
	 • Understandability

Elements	• **Revenue (expense)** Increase (decrease) in assets or decrease (increase) in liabilities from central operations. • **Gain (loss)** Increase (decrease) in assets or decrease (increase) in liabilities from peripheral operations. • **Other comprehensive income** Change in equity from nonowner sources. • **Asset** The result of a past transaction, owned today, a benefit in the future. • **Liability** The result of a past transaction, owed today, a sacrifice in the future. • **Equity** Owners' residual interest. Assets less liabilities. • **Investment by owner (distribution to owner)** Owner contribution to (withdrawal from) the company.
Concepts	• **Conservatism** Don't overstate assets or net income. • **Matching** Apply expense to revenue in period revenue is accrued, e.g., commission expense is applied in month of sale, not month of payment to employees. • **Historical cost** Most assets and liabilities are reported on basis of acquisition price because it is faithfully representative. But departure from historical cost is allowed when another measurement is more conservative (e.g., fair value is used for inventory, impairments) or more representative (e.g., present value of cash flows is used for long-term assets and liabilities). • **Accrual** Initial journal entry is adjusting entry on Balance Sheet date. Cash entry comes later. • **Deferral** Initial journal entry is for cash. Adjusting entry comes later on Balance Sheet date. • **Financial capital maintenance** GAAP. Aim is to maintain purchasing power, e.g., buy 10, sell 15, current cost 12 gain 5. • **Physical capital maintenance** Not GAAP. Aim is to maintain operating capacity, e.g., buy 10, sell 15, current cost 12, gain 3.

Revenue recognition
- ASC 606 *Revenue from Contracts with Customers* identifies the following core principle of revenue recognition: The entity recognizes revenue on the transfer of goods or services to the customer for an amount the entity contractually expects to receive.
- Revenue recognition is not triggered by the signing of the contract nor by customer payment. The entity recognizes revenue when it satisfies its **performance obligation** by transferring goods or services to the customer.
- Performance obligation is a contractual obligation to make delivery of goods or services.
  - A contract that calls for more than one good or service to be delivered may or may not consist of more than one performance obligation. To qualify as a distinct obligation, both of the following have to be true:
    - Customer can use the good or service on its own or with other readily available resources.
    - Good or service is separately identifiable from others in the contract.
- Performance obligation is satisfied at a point in time when customer obtains control of good or service. The following are indicators of the transfer of control:
  - Entity has present right to payment.
  - Entity has transferred physical possession to customer.
  - Customer has legal title.
  - Customer has significant risks and rewards of ownership.
  - Customer has accepted the asset.
- Performance obligation is satisfied over time when entity transfers control over time and one of the following is true:
  - Customer has control even as entity continues to create or enhance the asset, e.g., work in progress asset, software subscription.
  - Customer receives asset and consumes asset simultaneously, i.e., routine and recurring service like a cleaning service.
  - Entity creates an asset that does not have alternative use to entity (e.g., entity cannot sell to another customer because of contractual restrictions or practical limitations) and it has a right to payment for work completed to date.

Fair value measurement
- Use highest and best use. In other words, use whichever is highest, value in-use or value in-exchange, and use asset in principal or most advantageous market.
- Use price received to sell—exit price—excluding shipping costs unless location is attribute of asset.
  - Do not use price paid to replace—entry price.
- Fair value hierarchy

Level 1	•	Quoted-unadjusted prices of identical assets in active markets.
		○ Adjusted prices are classified in lower levels.
Level 2	•	Quoted prices of similar assets in active or inactive markets and market-corroborated inputs like interest rates.
Level 3	•	Unobservable inputs that approximate market participant assumptions.

Fair value option
- Fair value option (FVO) can only be applied at certain times. Here are the most common election dates:
  - Date item is first recognized.
  - Date investment has to use equity method of accounting.
  - Date item has to be remeasured (e.g., business combination).
- FVO cannot be elected for pensions, leases, consolidated subsidiaries, and financial instruments classified as stockholders' equity (e.g., share-based payments).
- FVO is irrevocable until a future election date, if any.
- FVO is elected for any allowed instrument, without applying to other identical instruments, except in a few cases most commonly:
  - If entity uses FVO instead of equity method, entity has to elect FVO for all other debt and equity investments in the investee (bonds held, preferred stock, etc).

Discontinued operations Component is disposed and disposal represents a strategic shift such that it has a major effect on financial condition or results of operations.
- Discontinued operations is reported on income statement after income from continuing operations.
  - Prior periods are amended on comparative financial statements. For consistency sake, operations gain or loss from subsequently discontinued operations should be shown as if they were discontinued at the start of the first period presented.
- Gain or loss from discontinued operations includes operations gain or loss, disposal gain or loss, insurance benefit and tax effect.
- To qualify as disposed, component has to be sold, discarded, or held for sale. This term *held for sale* is defined as all of the following:
  - Management commits to plan of disposal.
  - Assets are available for sale.
  - Active program to locate buyer.
  - Sale is probable.
  - Plan is very unlikely to change.

Comprehensive income

- Comprehensive income is the sum of net income and other comprehensive income. It is presented in one of the following ways:
  - At the bottom of the income statement.
  - In a separate statement directly after the income statement.

Temporary accounts	Net income gets closed to...		Other comprehensive income gets closed to...
Permanent accounts	...Retained earnings.		...Accumulated other comprehensive income.

- Chapter listings for items of other comprehensive income:
  - Chapter 6C
    - Projected benefit obligation gain or loss from change of pension formula, expected retirement age, life expectancy, or discount rate.
    - Plan assets gain or loss from difference between expected return and actual return.
  - Chapter 9
    - Unrealized holding gain or loss of available for sale security.
    - Impairment of available for sale security.
    - Impairment of held to maturity security.
    - Sale or reclassification of available for sale security—from reversal of unrealized holding gain or loss.
  - Chapter 12
    - Gain or loss on cash flow hedge.
  - Chapter 13C
    - Foreign currency gain or loss using translation method.

Disclosures

Significant accounting policies	Disclose in notes to financial statements: - State—do not describe—accounting principles and methods when there are GAAP alternatives, when the principles are specific to one industry (even those that are common practice within industry), and when the applications are unusual or innovative. - Examples include depreciation method, amortization of intangibles, valuation of inventory, revenue recognition for construction contracts and revenue recognition for franchising/leasing operations.
Related-party	For transactions with owners, management, families of both, affiliated companies, or equity-method investees, disclose in notes to financial statements. - Relationship to the company. - Description of transaction. - Dollar amount of transaction. - The following are not related-party transactions: officer salaries/expense allowances, intercompany sales.
Substantial doubt of going concern It is probable that company will not be able to pay current liabilities.	Disclose in notes to financial statements: - Conditions that are responsible for substantial doubt. - Ability to pay current liabilities. - Plans to mitigate substantial doubt.

Subsequent event Event occurs after balance sheet date and before financial statements are available to be issued.	Condition existed at BS date.	Condition did not exist at BS date.	Condition did not exist at BS date, but omission makes report unreliable.
	Recognize as adjustment to financial statements.	Do not report.	Disclose in notes to financial statements.
	ex. Bad debt expense, warranty expense, legal settlement for event that pre-existed.	ex. Sale of bond or CS, loss of assets from fire, foreign currency loss, legal settlement for event that did not pre-exist.	ex. Significant merger or legal settlement for event that did not pre-exist.

- For public company, subsequent event occurs after balance sheet date and before financial statements are issued.

Comparative financial statements
- Nonpublic company is not required to prepare comparative financial statements.
- Public company is required to prepare balance sheet for two prior years. It's also required to prepare income statement, statement of cash flows and statement of changes in equity for three prior years.

SEC reporting
- **Form 8-K** Information about material events, including all obvious ones, and changes in operations, changes in directors or CEO, changes in CPA or auditor, failure to (fill in the blank). File within 4 days of event.
- **Regulation Fair Disclosure** Simultaneous disclosure to all investors whenever registrant discloses, intentionally or not, any of its own material nonpublic information.
- **Regulation S-X** Instructions for financial statements.

	Non-accelerated filer < 75M	Accelerated filer ≥ 75M	Large accelerated filer ≥ 700M
10-K annual report (audited)	90 days after year end	75 days after year end	60 days after year end
10-Q quarterly report (not audited)	45 days after quarter end	40 days after quarter end	40 days after quarter end

GAAP	IFRS
• GAAP uses the term *net income* or *net loss*. • Expense classification and disclosure is not required. • Parenthetical disclosures (e.g., "net of allowance for uncollectible accounts") are reported on face of financials. • Balance sheet ordering starts with current assets. • Comparative financial statements are not required. • Statement of shareholders' equity may be presented as a separate statement or in the footnotes.	• IFRS uses the term *profit or loss for the period*. • Expense classification and disclosure is required. • Parenthetical disclosures are reported in notes to financial statements. • Balance sheet does not have ordering. • Comparative financial statements are required for prior year. • Statement of shareholders' equity must be presented as a separate statement.

2. Accounting Changes and Errors

Understated True balance is higher.
Overstated True balance is lower.

Accounting changes

Change in principle	Change in reporting entity	Change in estimate
ex. Change in inventory methods, change in construction method.	ex. Subsidiary enters (leaves) bankruptcy, subsidiary loses (regains) control to foreign company.	ex. Change in depreciation method, change in salvage value, change in useful life, change in bad debt expense.
• Retrospective approach • In earliest year presented, adjust assets and liabilities by the cumulative effect of accounting change, and adjust RE to balance. Repeat this in later years for year-specific effect.	• Retrospective approach • In all years presented, change financial statements to those of new entity.	• Prospective approach • In current year, use the new estimate.

- **Direct effects** Effects to assets, liabilities and impairment losses are included in computation of cumulative effect.
- **Indirect effects** Effects to current and future cash flows are excluded from computation of cumulative effect.
- If the company cannot determine the prior year effects of a change in principle, then retrospective approach is considered impracticable and prospective approach is used instead.

Errors To correct errors from previous years, company makes **prior period adjustment**. The steps are essentially the same as for a change in principle.

ex. During Year 3, Co. found two errors. Co. discovered ending inventory was understated by $6,000 in Year 1, and ending inventory was overstated by $2,500 in Year 2. Ignore taxes. Find the cumulative effect to retained earnings on 1/1/3.

		$6,000 understatement	$2,500 overstatement
Year 1	Beginning inventory Ending inventory Cost of goods sold Net income Retained earnings	True balance. True balance is 6,000 higher. True balance is 6,000 lower. True balance is 6,000 higher. True balance is 6,000 higher.	
Year 2	Beginning inventory Ending inventory Cost of goods sold Net income Retained earnings	True balance is 6,000 higher. True balance. True balance is 6,000 higher. True balance is 6,000 lower. True balance.	True balance. True balance is 2,500 lower. True balance is 2,500 higher. True balance is 2,500 lower. True balance is 2,500 lower.

- The $6,000 error self-corrects by the end of Year 2, so the only adjustment necessary on 1/1/3 is related to the $2,500 overstatement.

01/01/03	dr. Retained Earnings	2,500	
	cr. Inventory		2,500

ex. During Year 2, Co. discovered Year 1 ending inventory was understated by $10,000. Tax rate is 30%. Record the prior year adjustment.

01/01/02	dr. Inventory	10,000	
	cr. Retained earnings		7,000
	cr. Taxes payable		3,000

3A. Inventory

Inventory Tangible personal property to be used in production for sale, in production for sale, and held for sale.
- Current Asset

Terms

FOB shipping point Purchase occurs at shipping point. Buyer has title and inventory in transit.
FOB destination Purchase occurs at destination. Buyer has title and inventory on delivery.
- If buyer requests a refund, buyer decreases inventory and accounts payable at authorization of refund (not at shipping point or destination).

Perpetual system of inventory

01/01/01	dr. Inventory	1,000	
	cr. Accounts Payable		1,000

- When inventory is significant to company, it generally uses perpetual system of inventory. Inventory get recalculated after each sale, and there is no purchases account using perpetual system of inventory. This means that freight-in increases inventory directly, rather than through purchases. Likewise, purchase discounts and purchase returns and allowances both decrease inventory directly.

Periodic system of inventory

01/01/01	dr. Purchases	1,000	
	cr. Accounts Payable		1,000

- Company makes a physical count of inventory at year end, and subtracts this from cost of goods available for sale to get cost of goods sold.

Net purchases

+ Purchases
+ Freight-in
− Purchase discounts
− Purchase returns and allowances
= Net purchases

Cost of goods sold

+ Beginning inventory
+ Net purchases
= Cost of goods available for sale
− Ending inventory
= Cost of goods sold

Purchase commitment loss Items contracted to buy decrease in value and contract is noncancellable. Debit estimated loss and credit accrued loss. Recovery is allowed if market value rebounds.

Purchase discounts

Accounting events:
1. Co. records purchase.
2. Co. takes purchase discount.
3. Alternatively, Co. does not take purchase discount.

Gross method

1.	dr. Purchases	1,000	cr. Accounts payable	1,000
2.	dr. Accounts payable	1,000	cr. Cash	980
			cr. Purchase discounts	20
3.	dr. Accounts payable	1,000	cr. Cash	1,000

Net method

dr. Purchases	980	cr. Accounts payable	980
dr. Accounts payable	980	cr. Cash	980
dr. Accounts payable	980	cr. Cash	1,000
dr. Purchase discounts lost	20		

- Under the gross method, purchase discounts is a contra expense to purchases.
- Under the gross method, purchase discounts not taken is a product cost (included in inventory). Under the net method, purchase discounts not taken is a period cost (not included in inventory).

Cost basis for pricing inventory

ex. Given the following inventory information, find COGS using Average Cost, FIFO and LIFO for both periodic and perpetual systems.

Date	Units	Unit cost	Total cost
1/1	300	1.30	390
1/10	200	1.40	280
1/14	Sell 350		
1/20	400	1.50	600
1/25	100	1.60	160

Perpetual method

Moving average Find all before sale.			
1/1	300	1.30	390
1/10	200	1.40	280

Average cost = 670 / 500 = 1.34
COGS = 350 × 1.34 = 469

FIFO Find first before sale.			
1/1	300	1.30	390
1/10	50	1.40	70

COGS = 390 + 70 = 460

LIFO Find last before sale.			
1/10	200	1.40	280
1/1	150	1.30	195

COGS = 280 + 195 = 475

Periodic method

Weighted average Find all of period.			
1/1	300	1.30	390
1/10	200	1.40	280
1/20	400	1.50	600
1/25	100	1.60	160

Average cost = 1,430 / 1,000 = 1.43
COGS = 350 × 1.43 = 500.50

FIFO Find first of period.			
1/1	300	1.30	390
1/10	50	1.40	70

COGS = 390 + 70 = 460

LIFO Find last of period.			
1/25	100	1.60	160
1/20	250	1.50	375

COGS = 160 + 375 = 535

Note

To get ending inventory, subtract COGS from COGAS. COGAS is uniform for all of the above calculations. In this case, since there is no beginning inventory, COGAS is equal to net purchases, $1,430.

- Assuming rising costs, LIFO has higher COGS because the most recent therefore higher inventory is treated as sold. Higher COGS means lower net income. FIFO is the opposite.
- LIFO produces an accurate income statement because you record the most recent costs (last in) against the revenues. On the other hand, FIFO produces an accurate balance sheet because you record the older costs (first in) against the revenues leaving the more recent costs in inventory.
- LIFO conformity rule: if LIFO is used in tax filing, then it must be used in financial reporting.

Dollar-value LIFO

ex. Given the following inventory information, find the LIFO inventory value.

Year	EI at end of year prices	Price index
1	2,000	1.00
2	2,760	1.20
3	3,125	1.25
4	3,185	1.30

Year	EI at end of year prices	EI at base year prices	Layers	EI at dollar-value LIFO
1	2,000	2,000 / 1.00 = 2,000	Year 1 = 2,000	+ 2,000 = 2,000
2	2,760	2,760 / 1.20 = 2,300	Year 1 = 2,000 Year 2 = 2,300 − 2,000 = 300	+ 2,000 + 300 × 1.20 = 2,360
3	3,125	3,125 / 1.25 = 2,500	Year 1 = 2,000 Year 2 = 2,300 − 2,000 = 300 Year 3 = 2,500 − 2,300 = 200	+ 2,000 + 300 × 1.20 + 200 × 1.25 = 2,610
4	3,185	3,185 / 1.30 = 2,450	Year 1 = 2,000 Year 2 = 2,300 − 2,000 = 300 Year 3 = 2,500 − 2,300 = 200 Year 4 = 2,450 − 2,500 = (50)	+ 2,000 + 300 × 1.20 + **150** × 1.25 + 0 × 1.30 = 2,547.50

Inventory impairment Inventory is valued at cost to start with. But once there is a decrease in value, inventory is written down to either NRV or Market. The entry for impairment is:

dr. COGS/Loss from market decline
　　cr. Inventory

Impairment for FIFO inventory and average cost methods	Impairment for LIFO inventory methods
Inventory is written down to lower of cost or net realizable value (LCNRV), where net realizable value is selling price less cost of completion less cost to sell.	Inventory is written down to lower of cost or market, where market is replacement cost. But the calculation is more involved than that because market cannot be above NRV (ceiling) nor below NRV less normal profit (floor).

Consignments

Consignor	Consignee AKA sales agent
• Title and inventory stay with consignor until sold to customer. • Record consignee sales commission as selling expense.	• Record consignee sales commission as other revenues and gains.

• On shipment to the consignee/sales, consignor does not record sale. • On sale, consignee sales commission is a selling expense of consignor (does not affect consignor net sales).

GAAP	IFRS
• Inventory valued at lower of cost or market or NRV. • One or more cost formulas are permitted for inventories with similar use. • LIFO method is permitted. • Impairment reversal is prohibited.	• Inventory valued at lower of cost or NRV. • Only one cost formula is permitted for inventories with similar use. • LIFO method is prohibited. • Impairment reversal to NRV is permitted.

3B. Construction Accounting

Construction in progress Inventory account that is used similar to how a merchant debits inventory after a purchase. A contractor debits this account many times over the course of the year, as costs are incurred.

- Construction in progress (CIP) differs from merchant inventory account in that contractor does not credit when he or she bills the customer. Instead, contractor credits billings account, which is a contra CIP account.
- **Percentage of completion method** Contractor makes an additional debit to CIP at year end. The debit is for current year gross profit. In effect, gross profit has increased the asset value.

> **Note**
>
> Use the following formula to start. Cumulative Revenue = (Cumulative Cost / Estimated Total Cost) × Contract Price. The rest is easy to solve. To get current year revenue, subtract all previous year revenue. Then to get gross profit, subtract cost.

ex. Contract price $1,000. Job is complete in Year 3. Please note all figures—including estimated future cost—are as of the end of the year.

	Year 1	Year 2	Year 3
Cost	200	300	430
Estimated future cost	700	410	0
Billings	175	320	505
Collections	150	310	540

— For percentage of completion method, make the following calculations.

	Year 1	Year 2	Year 3
Cumulative cost	200	200 + 300 = 500	200 + 300 + 430 = 930
Estimated total cost	200 + 700 = 900	500 + 410 = 910	930 + 0 = 930
Cumulative revenue	(200 / 900) × 1,000 = 222	(500 / 910) × 1,000 = 549	(930 / 930) × 1,000 = 1,000
Revenue	222 − 0 = 222	549 − 222 = 327	1,000 − 549 = 451

— Both methods have identical journal entries to start. Mnemonic for the first three journal entries for both methods: C CAR B CAR.

Year 1

dr. **CIP**	200	cr. **Cash**	200
dr. **AR**	175	cr. **Billings**	175
dr. **C**ash	150	cr. **AR**	150

Year 2

dr. CIP	300	cr. Cash	300
dr. AR	320	cr. Billings	320
dr. Cash	310	cr. AR	310

Year 3

dr. CIP	430	cr. Cash	430
dr. AR	505	cr. Billings	505
dr. Cash	540	cr. AR	540

— For the percentage of completion method, you need additional journal entries as follows.

dr. Expense	200	cr. Revenue	222
dr. CIP	22		

dr. Expense	300	cr. Revenue	327
dr. CIP	27		

dr. Expense	430	cr. Revenue	451
dr. CIP	21		

dr. Billings	1,000	cr. CIP	1,000

— For the completed contract method, you need additional journal entries as follows. This method is used when cost estimates cannot be made. Without estimates, there's nothing extra to be done until the year of completion.

dr. Expense	930	cr. Revenue	70
dr. CIP	1,000		

dr. Billings	1,000	cr. CIP	1,000

4. Operational Assets

Operational asset Noncurrent asset that is used in the production of goods and services. There are two categories of operational assets.

Fixed asset AKA property, plant and equipment	• Noncurrent • Nonmonetary	ex. Land, Buildings, Equipment, Machinery, Autos, Trucks.
Intangible asset	• Noncurrent • Nonmonetary	ex. Patents, Copyrights, Trademarks, Software, Goodwill, Leaseholds, Organization costs, Research and development costs, Franchises.

Fixed asset

Capitalize to fixed asset	Capitalize to land
All costs to put item into use. ex. Price, sales tax, shipping, permits, interest on constructing asset, excavation of foundation, asset retirement obligations.	All costs before ready to construct. ex. Land price, broker fees, title fees, transfer taxes, back property taxes, demolition of old building net of salvage proceeds, clearing, grading.

• Lower of actual interest or avoidable interest. After asset is substantially complete, interest is expensed. Also, interest on purchasing asset is expensed. • An example of asset retirement obligation is shown in Chapter 5.

- Post-acquisition expenditure is capitalized if the asset becomes more productive or asset useful life is extended.
  - The estimate of the asset's useful life includes a minimum level of repairs and maintenance. Ordinary repairs and maintenance are already built into the estimate because without that the estimate would be trivial (car would have a useful life of 3,000 miles, etc). As a result, repairs and maintenance do not increase the useful life and should be expensed in the period incurred.
  - Generally, if an expenditure is capitalized, it will be depreciated over the shorter of it's useful life or the remaining useful life of the larger asset.
    - There's an exception for an addition that is not an integral part of the larger asset. In this case, depreciate over the addition's useful life.

Exchange of fixed asset
- Gain and loss is based on the asset given up. Loss is recognized in full. Gain is also recognized in full as long as as the exchange has commercial substance—in that it changes future cash flows for the two parties. Unfortunately, recognition is more involved for one subset of gain transactions, gain without commercial substance.

- **Gain without commercial substance**

Co. does not give or receive cash.	Co. gives cash.	Co. receives cash
Co. does not recognize any gain.	Co. does not recognize any gain.	Co. recognizes partial gain proportional to cash ratio. $\dfrac{\text{Cash in}}{\text{Cash in + FV other assets in}} * \text{Total Gain}$

• Cash ratio above 25% triggers full gain recognition.

- Basis of new asset = Fair value of asset given up − Boot received + Boot paid + Deferred gain

Depreciation
- Depreciation for asset in showroom is selling expense, for asset in factory is COGS, and for asset in corporate headquarters is G&A expense.
- Depreciate intangibles using straight-line method over shorter of useful life or legal life.
- Depreciation base for all methods except double declining balance = Historical cost − Salvage value
- Depreciation base for double declining balance = Historical cost − Accumulated depreciation

ex. Historical cost is $1,000. Salvage value is $100. Useful life is 5 years. Estimated output is 1,000 units. Actual Year 1 output is 250 units, and actual Year 2 output is 300 units.

	Straight line	Double declining balance	Physical usage	Sum of years
Co. purchases fixed asset on 1/1.	Y1 = 900 × (1/5) Y2 = 900 × (1/5)	Y1 = **1,000** × (2/5) Y2 = **600** × (2/5)	Y1 = 900 × (250/1,000) Y2 = 900 × (300/1,000)	Y1 = 900 × (5/15) Y2 = 900 × (4/15)
Co. purchases fixed asset on 7/1.	Y1 = 900 × (1/5) × (1/2) Y2 = 900 × (1/5)	Y1 = 1,000 × (2/5) × (1/2) Y2 = 800 × (2/5)	Y1 = 900 × (250/1,000) Y2 = 900 × (300/1,000)	Y1 = 900 × (5/15) × (1/2) Y2 = 900 × (5/15) × (1/2) + 900 × (4/15) × (1/2)

General intangibles

- Acquired
  - Capitalize purchase price, legal fees, and filing fees if one of the following is true:
    - Intangible is acquired legally or by contract.
    - Intangible is separable: it can be separated and exchanged, rented, sold, etc.
- Internally developed
  - Expense costs related to internal development of intangibles including organization costs and research and development costs.
    - Likewise, expense the cost of developing a patent. The only cost that should be capitalized is the cost of registering a patent including filing fees, engineer fees, attorney fees and fees for successful defense of patent.

Internally developed software

1. Expense as research and development costs up to tech feasibility.
2. Capitalize costs up to general release. Amortize greater of S/L method or current revenue/total estimated revenue.
3. Inventory the production costs and expense as cost of goods sold.

Research and development costs

- Generally, research and development (R&D) costs are not capitalized.
- Fixed assets used in R&D is an exception to this general rule:
  - When fixed asset is acquired for more than one R&D project…
    - Capitalize fixed asset.
    - Instead of depreciation expense, debit research and development expense and credit accumulated depreciation.
  - When fixed asset is repurposed for one R&D project from elsewhere in company…
    - Fixed asset is already capitalized.
    - Instead of depreciation expense, debit research and development expense and credit accumulated depreciation.
  - When fixed asset is acquired for one R&D project and has no other use…
    - Expense fixed asset.
      - Even though asset has a useful life greater than one year, fixed asset is expensed because this is consistent with most R&D costs.
- The following keywords indicate the cost in question is not R&D: commercial, seasonal, routine, quality control, adaptation, troubleshooting.

Impairment loss

	Test for loss	Calculate loss	Depreciate after?	Write up after?
Tangible held to use	CV > Nondiscounted CF	CV – FV	Yes	No
Tangible held for sale	CV > NRV	CV – NRV	No	Yes
Intangible finite life	CV > Nondiscounted CF	CV – FV	Yes	No
Intangible indefinite life	CV > FV	CV – FV	No	No
Goodwill	CV reporting unit with goodwill > FV reporting unit with goodwill	CV reporting unit with goodwill – FV reporting unit with goodwill	No	No

- For public company, impairment loss is reported as operating expenses. For nonpublic company, impairment loss is reported as other expenses.

GAAP	IFRS
- Interest income from construction loan is prohibited from offsetting interest cost. - Accounting estimates are not reviewed annually—estimates are changed as needed. - Component depreciation is not required for fixed asset made of individual components with varying lives. - Fixed asset is prohibited from revaluation to fair value. (Tangible asset held for sale does get write up but gain is capped at the amount of the impairment loss.) - Impairment test for intangible uses **undiscounted** cash flows. - Impairment on intangible is prohibited from write up.	- Interest income from construction loan is permitted to offset interest cost. - Accounting estimates are reviewed annually for changes in useful life, salvage value and depreciation method. - Component depreciation is required for fixed asset made of individual components with varying lives. - Fixed asset is permitted to revalue to fair value—given reliable measurement (i.e., there is an active market). Election to revalue applies to entire class of assets. - Impairment test for intangible uses **discounted** cash flows to determine *recoverable amount.* - Impairment on intangible is permitted to write up.

5. Monetary Current Assets and Liabilities

- **Monetary asset** Claim to receive cash in amounts fixed or determinable without reference to future prices.
- **Monetary liability** Obligation to pay cash in amounts fixed or determinable without reference to future prices.

- **Nonmonetary asset**
  - Claim to receive cash in amounts dependent on future prices.
  - Goods held primarily for resale or direct use.
- **Nonmonetary liability**
  - Obligation to pay cash in amounts dependent on future prices.
  - Obligation to furnish all goods or services.

Terms

- **Cash equivalent** Financial instrument with an original maturity of 3 months or fewer.
- **Compensating balance** Money that must stay on deposit with bank as a condition of the loan. ex. If borrower must keep $2,000 compensating balance as condition of $10,000 loan at 6%, then only $8,000 borrowed and interest payment of $600 has 7.5% effective interest rate. Disclose all compensating balances.
- **Restricted cash** Cash set aside to comply with agreement or for future use.

The following are cash equivalents:
- Certificate of deposit, no penalty or immaterial penalty - Compensating balance, unrestricted or immaterial restriction - Treasury bill - Money market fund - Commercial paper

The following are not cash equivalents:

- Certificate of deposit, material penalty
- Compensating balance, material restriction
- Treasury note, treasury bond
- Restricted cash, e.g., sinking fund, dividend fund, payroll fund

Bank reconciliation

Balance per bank	Balance per books
+ Outstanding checks − Outstanding deposits + − Error on bank statement	− Unrecorded customer NSF check − Unrecorded bank charges + Unrecorded note collected by bank directly + − Error on books
Corrected cash balance per books	Corrected cash balance per books

Accounts receivable is reported at net realizable value, meaning that it's reported in the assets section and then allowance for doubtful accounts is stated directly beneath it. The allowance account is an offset to gross accounts receivable and the difference (the net amount) is shown.

- **Bad debt expense**
  - Allowance method is the only acceptable method for recording bad debt expense.
  - Direct write-off method is not GAAP because bad debt expense is not recorded in the same period as revenue.

Accounting events:
1. Co. records revenue of $2,000.
2. Co. estimates uncollectible accounts of $150.
3. Co. writes off uncollectible accounts $50.
4. Co. collects a previously written-off account of $25.

Allowance method

1.	dr. Accounts receivable	2,000	cr. Revenue	2,000
2.	dr. Bad debt expense	150	cr. Allowance	150
3.	dr. Allowance	50	cr. Accounts receivable	50
4.	dr. Accounts receivable dr. Cash	25 25	cr. Allowance cr. Accounts receivable	25 25

Direct write-off method

dr. Accounts receivable	2,000	cr. Revenue	2,000
dr. Bad debt expense	50	cr. Accounts receivable	50
dr. Accounts receivable dr. Cash	25 25	cr. Bad debt expense cr. Accounts receivable	25 25

Allowance for uncollectible accounts For reporting on the balance sheet, use one of the following methods to calculate the allowance for uncollectible accounts—which we refer to below as ending balance. Both are acceptable GAAP.

Income statement approach

— Calculate bad debt expense then solve for ending balance.
— Bad Debt Expense = Sales × Bad Debt %

Allowance for uncollectible accounts

Write-offs	Beginning balance Bad debt expense (Calc) Recoveries
	Ending balance (**Plug**)

Balance sheet approach

— Calculate ending balance directly.
— Ending Balance = Age Group 1 × Uncollectible 1 % + Age Group 2 × Uncollectible 2 % + …

Allowance for uncollectible accounts

Write-offs	Beginning balance Bad debt expense (Plug) Recoveries
	Ending balance (**Calc**)

Financing with receivables

- There are two broad categories of financing with receivables. The transaction is either a sale of receivables or a secured borrowing.

Sale of receivables Defined as all of the following:
- Transfer cannot be avoided in bankruptcy.
- Transferee has the right to sell or borrow against assets.
- No agreement in place to repurchase or return assets.

Factoring Company sells receivables for cash. Receives most cash up front, then the balance once receivables collected. Minus fee to factor. And minus uncollectible receivables if sold with recourse.

Securitization Company sells pool of receivables and loans from the company to special purpose entity. Entity then issues bonds or other securities that are secured by this pool.

Secured borrowing Fails one of the sales criteria.

Assigning Company borrows from bank with specific receivables as security.

Pledging Company borrows from bank with receivables in general as security. Same accounting treatment as assigning.

Factoring ex.

Co. has total AR of $145,000. Factors $100,000 to bank with recourse. Bank charges 2% fee. Bank pays Co. $90,000 up front and agrees to pay $8,000 (that's $10,000 balance − 2% fee) once collected.

Factoring with recourse, internally estimated at 5% of AR

dr. Cash 90,000
dr. Loss on sale 2,000 + 5,000
dr. Receivable from factor 8,000
    cr. Liability 5,000
    cr. AR 100,000

Factoring without recourse

dr. Cash 90,000
dr. Loss on sale 2,000
dr. Receivable from factor 8,000
    cr. Liability
    cr. AR 100,000

Assigning ex.

Co. has total AR of $145,000. On 1/1/1, assigns $120,000 to bank. Bank charges 12% interest on loan of $100,000, and charges fee equal to 2% of AR assigned. By 12/31/1, $50,000 of AR collected.

1/1/1 Co. records assignment.	dr. Cash 97,600 dr. Assignment expense 2,400 cr. Liability 100,000
12/31/1 Co. collects AR.	dr. Cash 50,000 cr. AR 50,000
12/31/1 Co. pays interest and pay down assignment.	dr. Liability 50,000 dr. Interest expense 12,000 cr. Cash 62,000

Terms

- **Loan participation** Several banks join in to fund one large loan.
- **Bankers acceptance** On behalf of retailer, retailer's bank issues a promise to pay to wholesale supplier. At some future date, bank will pay holder (in this case, wholesale supplier) and will recoup directly from retailer's bank account. This instrument is potentially useful to retailer, who couldn't have bought on credit. Retailer may even be able to resell the goods before instrument comes due.

Payroll tax liability

- Employer must withhold the employee's income tax and the employee's share of FICA tax. Withholdings are liabilities to the employer until it deposits that money to government (deadline for deposit depends on size of employer, large employer could have 1 day to deposit while small one could have the whole quarter).
  - Although these withholdings are liabilities to the employer, they are expenses to employee. So payroll expense does not change even if there is a change to one of its components—the offset is to net paycheck and payroll expense remains the same.
- Employer must pay employer share of FICA tax and unemployment tax. These are liabilities to the employer as well as expenses to the employer. Payroll tax expense does change if there is a change to one of its components.

Payroll expense	Components
dr. Payroll expense	cr. Federal income tax payable cr. State income tax payable cr. Employee FICA tax payable cr. Net paycheck (Plug)

Payroll tax expense	Components
dr. Payroll tax expense	cr. Employer FICA tax payable cr. Federal unemployment tax payable cr. State unemployment tax payable

Optional expenses to employer electing fringe benefits...	
dr. 401K expense dr. Health insurance expense	cr. Employer match 401k payable cr. Employer health insurance payable

...but no employer tax expense for these fringe benefits.

- Large employers with at least 50 employees are required to offer health coverage—but still not required to subsidize any portion of it. • If employer elects to pay some of the premium on behalf of employee—or to match employee 401K contributions—this amount is the expense to the employer. Amounts paid by the employee are additional components of payroll expense which lower net paycheck.

Compensated absences

ex. During the year, employee accumulates $2,500 vacation pay and uses $2,000. At year end, Co. records the following journal entry:

12/31 Co. accrues salary expense.	dr. Salary expense	500	cr. Liability—absences	500

- For holiday and vacation pay, salary expense accrues when all of the following are true:
  - Service is performed as of balance sheet date.
  - Benefits accumulate (benefits carry to future years) or vest (benefits pay upon departure or retirement).
  - Payment is probable.
  - Payment is reasonably estimated.
- For accumulated benefits, if the company estimates that 10% of benefits are never paid, then only 90% is accrued to begin with.
- Sick pay has to be vested to accrue.

Litigation

	Known	Reasonably estimable	Not reasonably estimable
Probable (> 70%)	Recognize and disclose	Recognize and disclose	Disclose
Reasonably possible	Disclose	Disclose	Disclose
Remote	Do not report	Do not report	Do not report

- Recognize and disclose
  - Recognize and disclose best estimate for range of loss. If no best estimate, recognize low end and disclose high end.
  - Recognize and disclose contingency even if lawsuit not yet filed, but likelihood of filing is probable.
- Disclose
  - Disclose if lose ruling, but likelihood of loss on appeal is still believed to be reasonably possible or remote.
  - Disclose all gain contingency. Disclosure should state likelihood of gain.
  - Disclose the following contingencies even if likelihood is remote: guarantees of other's debt, standby letters of credit by bank, agreements to repurchase receivables.
- Do not report
  - Do not report if cause of loss contingency does not occur before statement date.
  - Do not report for risk of fire or catastrophe, and general business risks.

Warranties

- There are two types of warranties: assurance-type and service-type. Only the service-type warranty is a separate performance obligation, and as a result it receives separate accounting treatment.

    ex. On 1/1/1, Co. records $100,000 sales for a product with two year service-type warranty. To the warranty, Co. has allocated $5,000 out of the $100,000 in sales. Past experience indicates 1% warranty payments during Year 1 and additional 2% warranty payments during Year 2.

1/1/1 Co. records sale and warranty liability.	dr. Cash or accounts receivable	100,000	cr. Sales cr. Unearned warranty revenue	95,000 5,000
12/31/1 Co. makes warranty payments of only $750 during Year 1.	dr. Warranty expense dr. Unearned warranty revenue	750 1,250	cr. Cash or inventory cr. Warranty revenue	750 1,250

- Warranty revenue in Year 1 = (750 / 3,000) × 5,000 = $1,250. (This is the weighted-average method for calculating revenue, but the straight-line method, whereby Co. recognizes revenue of $750, is also acceptable.) ● For Year 2, warranty expense is still just the actual warranty payments. But warranty revenue in Year 2 is the final $3,750 because the performance obligation has been completed.

Asset retirement obligations

    ex. Co. builds $300M gas facility to last 10 years. Expects to pay $15M in Year 10 to decommission. Let's assume PV of decommission is $9M.

1/1/1 Co. builds facility.	dr. Gas facility	309M	cr. Cash cr. Asset retirement obligation	300M 9M
12/31/1 Co. records depreciation of facility.	dr. Depreciation expense		cr. Accumulated depreciation	
12/31/1 Co. records accretion expense (interest expense) because one less year to retirement.	dr. Accretion expense		cr. Asset retirement obligation	

Ratios

- **Current ratio** Current assets / Current liabilities
- **Quick ratio** Cash and cash equivalents, Net receivables, and Short term investments / Current liabilities
    - Quick ratio excludes the following from numerator: inventory, prepaid items, and available for sale securities.

	Accounts Payable	Inventory	Accounts Receivable
Turnover	Purchases / Average AP	COGS / Average Inventory	Sales / Average AR
Conversion period	Average AP / (Purchases / 365)	Average Inventory / (COGS / 365)	Average AR / (Sales / 365)
Days outstanding	Ending AP / (Purchases / 365)	Ending Inventory / (COGS / 365)	Ending AR / (Sales / 365)

- Alternatively, turnover is calculated using ending AP (or inventory or AR) in denominator. ● In practice, turnover is greater than 1, which means turnover decreases when numerator and denominator increase by same amount, e.g., end of year sale causes AR turnover to decrease.

GAAP	IFRS
<ul><li>Short term obligation is permitted to reclassify to noncurrent if company has intent and ability to refinance.</li><li>*Contingent liability* refers to all uncertain future loss—both loss that is disclosed only and loss that is recognized (i.e., accrued) and disclosed.</li><li>Criteria for loss recognition: likelihood is probable (greater than 70%).</li></ul>	<ul><li>Short term obligation is permitted to reclassify to noncurrent only if company enters into agreement to refinance.</li><li>*Contingent liability* refers to uncertain future loss that is disclosed only. *Provision* refers to uncertain future loss that is recognized and disclosed.</li><li>Criteria for loss recognition: more likely than not (greater than 50%).</li></ul>

6A. Time Value, Notes and Bonds

Terms

Ordinary annuity Funds paid at end of period AKA annuity in arrears.
Annuity due Funds paid at beginning of period AKA annuity in advance.
Market rate of interest AKA real rate, yield, yield to market, effective rate.
Contract rate of interest AKA coupon rate, stated rate, bond rate, face rate, nominal rate.
Term financing Principal matures in entirety on single date. Calls for level interest payments.
Serial financing Principal matures in segments on many dates. Calls for level principal or level combined payments, e.g., level combined payments in real estate financing.
Bond discount Contra liability, normal debit, reported in the liability section of the BS such that it decreases the liability.
Bond premium Adjunct liability, normal credit, reported in the liability section of the BS such that it increases the liability.

Time value

- Time value concepts are most commonly tested (1) to value term bonds (2) to value serial leases.
- Given a present cash asset, you can calculate the future value. Or given a future cash asset, you can calculate the present value.
  - Future value = Present value $\times (1 + i)^n$
    Present value = Future value $\times (1 / (1 + i)^n)$
    where $\quad$ i = Interest rate per period (e.g., 10% interest/year = 5% interest/half year)
    $\qquad\qquad$ n = Number of periods
- The term $(1 + i)^n$ is a time value of money factor (TVMF) that is used to calculate future value. Likewise, the term $1 / (1 + i)^n$ is a TVMF that is used to calculate present value. TVMF may take the form of a formula like $1 / (1 + .06)^2$ or equivalent real number .89000. There is a unique TVMF for each combination of interest rate and number of periods.
- In practice, we mainly need to calculate present value using PV TVMF and PVA TVMF for an annuity.

ex. Find PV of $20 transfer in period 10. Interest rate is 4%. PV = FV of single sum × PV TVMF PV = 20 × PV TVMF (10, 4%) = 20 × .67556 = 13.51	ex. Find PVA of $20 transfers for next 10 periods. Interest rate is 4%. PVA = FV of periodic payments × PVA TVMF PVA = 20 × PVA TVMF (10, 4%) = 20 × 8.11090 = 162.22

- PVA TVMF = (1 - PV TVMF) / i
- PV TVMF (1, X%) + PV TVMF (2, X%) = PVA TVMF (2, X%)
- Ordinary annuity TVMF × (1 + i) = Annuity due TVMF

Notes payable

- Notes can be serial or term. We present a serial note payable with a series of level total payments that cover both interest and principal.

  ex. Co. issues a $100,000 note payable. Matures in 5 years. Market interest rate is 6%. How much are even total payments?

  — Find the PVA TVMF. $\qquad\qquad$ PVA TVMF (5, 6%) = 4.21236
  — Find the amount of payments. $\qquad$ PVA = FV of periodic payments × PVA TVMF
  $\qquad\qquad\qquad\qquad\qquad\qquad$ 100,000 = FV of periodic payments × 4.21236
  $\qquad\qquad\qquad\qquad\qquad\qquad$ FV of even total payments = 23,739.66

Year	Payment	Interest expense	Change in book value	Book value
1/1/1				100,000.00
12/31/1	23,739.66	6,000 (100,000 × .06)	17,739.66	82,260.34
12/31/2	23,739.66	4,935.62 (82,260.34 × .06)	18,804.04	63,456.30

- Notes payable balance always approaches what is owed at maturity, in this case $0.
- Non-interest bearing note is not how it sounds. It is not when a family member loans you $5,000, and you agree to repay $5,000 in 2 years at no interest. It gets its name because it does not have stated interest rate on its face. But you do pay interest, an implied interest which is the difference between how much you receive initially and how much you must pay at maturity. ex. Bank loans you just $4,500 but you need to pay the $5,000 face value at maturity.

1/1/1 Co. issues note.	dr. Cash	100,000.00	cr. Note payable	100,000.00
12/31/1 Co. pays interest.	dr. Interest expense dr. Note payable	6,000.00 17,739.66	cr. Cash	23,739.66

Bonds payable Bonds can be serial or term. We present a term bond payable since it is more common. This type of bond provides for a series of level interest payments at a contract rate of interest and the face value of bond is due at maturity.

　ex. Co. issues $10,000 bond payable. Matures in 5 years. Semiannual interest payments of 8% on 6/1 and 1/1. Market interest rate is 6%.

　— Find PV of principal amount. 10,000.00 × PV TVMF (10, 3%) = 10,000.00 × .74409 = 7,440.90
　— Find PVA of interest payments. 400.00 × PVA TVMF (10, 3%) = 400.00 × 8.53020 = 3,412.08
　— Value bonds payable. PV of principal amount + PVA of interest payments = 7,440.90 + 3,412.08 = 10,852.98

Year	Payment	Interest expense	Change in book value	Book value
1/1/1				10,852.98
6/30/1	400.00 (10,000 × .04)	325.59 (10,852.98 × .03)	74.41	10,778.57
12/31/1	400.00 (10,000 × .04)	323.36 (10,778.57 × .03)	76.64	10,701.93

● Book value always approaches what is owed at maturity. ● Use effective interest method for amortization—unless interest is immaterial, then straight line method is also acceptable.

　ex. Same facts as above, but bond issuance is one month late. Since the bond covenant calls for a full interest payment on 6/30, Co. collects the previous month of interest from the purchaser, records a liability, then returns it with the full interest payment on 6/30.

2/1/1 Co. issues bond.	dr. Cash	10,852.98 + 66.67	cr. Bonds payable cr. Bonds premium cr. Interest payable	10,000.00 852.98 66.67
6/30/1 Co. pays interest.	dr. Interest expense dr. Bond premium dr. Interest payable	325.59 − 66.67 74.41 66.67	cr. Cash	400.00

　ex. Same facts as above, but use 2/28 year end.

2/28/1 Co. accrues two additional months of interest expense at year end.	dr. Interest expense dr. Bonds premium	108.53 (325.59 × 2/6) 24.80 (74.41 × 2/6)	cr. Interest payable	133.33 (400.00 × 2/6)
6/30/1 Co. accrues final four months and pays semiannual interest payment.	dr. Interest expense dr. Bonds premium dr. Interest payable	217.06 (325.59 × 4/6) 49.61 (74.41 × 4/6) 133.33	cr. Cash	400.00

Debt issue costs Costs in connection with issuing bonds, including legal, accounting, printing, registration, and underwriting fees. Reported in Other assets on balance sheet. Debt issue costs is reported in liabilities section as adjustment to bond payable—just like bond premium and bond discount.

　ex. Same facts as above, but debt issue costs of $100.

1/1/1 Co. issues bond.	dr. Cash dr. Debt issue costs	10,752.98 100.00	cr. Bonds payable cr. Bonds premium	10,000.00 852.98
6/30/1 Co. pays interest.	dr. Interest expense dr. Bond premium	322.59 77.41	cr. Cash	400.00

● Once issued, debt issue costs is combined with bond premium/discount and amortization table is reconstructed with $10,752.98 initial balance.

Loan origination

	Effect on lender	Effect on borrower
Loan origination fee	Lender deducts from principal, recording income gradually over loan.	Borrower deducts from principal, recording expense gradually over loan.
Loan origination cost	Lender adds to principal, recording expense gradually over loan.	

● Lender is also subject to indirect loan origination costs. While these costs are somewhat related to the loan, they would be incurred with or without a loan. Lender expenses these costs as soon as they are incurred.

6B. Debt Restructure

- **Debt settlement** Creditor settles the debt outright at time of restructuring. Debtor's gain on settlement equals creditor's loss.
- **Modification of terms** In this type of debt restructure, creditor allows debt to continue but reduces/delays interest payments or reduces/delays maturity amount. Debtor's gain on modification does not equal creditor's loss.

Debt settlement

ex. On 1/1/3, creditor agrees to settle $50,000 note receivable and $2,000 interest receivable in exchange for property having a fair value of $40,000 and a carrying value on debtor's books of $35,000.

Creditor

1/1/3	dr. Land	40,000	cr. Note receivable	50,000
	dr. Loss on settlement	12,000	cr. Interest receivable	2,000

Debtor

1/1/3	dr. Land	5,000	cr. Gain on sale	5,000
	dr. Note payable	50,000	cr. Gain on settlement	12,000
	dr. Interest payable	2,000	cr. Land	40,000

Modification of terms Debtor

- When total future cash payments are less than carrying value, debtor records gain and debtor does not record interest expense—future payments decrease principal.
- When total future cash payments are more than carrying value, debtor does not record gain and debtor records interest expense using a new rate.

ex. Creditor issued a term note to debtor for $20,000, and debtor can't make the $2,000 interest payment for the year just ended. According to the note, debtor also needs to make two subsequent $2,000 payments at year end for each of two remaining years to maturity, as well as pay the maturity amount of $20,000. Carrying value is $22,000 ($20,000 maturity amount + $2,000 accrued interest). Market rate of interest is 8%.

Total future cash payments are less than carrying value.

Creditor agrees to forgive accrued interest, to decrease principal to $19,000, and forgive final year's $2,000.

— Find gain.
Gain = Carrying value − Total future cash payments
Gain = 22,000 − 21,000 = 1,000

1/1/1 Co. records gain.	dr. Notes payable 1,000
	cr. Gain on modification 1,000
12/31/1 Co. makes payment.	dr. Notes payable 2,000
	cr. Cash 2,000
12/31/2 Co. settles debt at maturity.	dr. Notes payable 19,000
	cr. Cash 19,000

Total future cash payments are more than carrying value.

Creditor agrees to accept $24,024 at maturity.

— Find new interest rate.
PV TVMF (2, i) = 22,000 / 24,024 = .91575
i ≅ 4.5%

12/31/1 Co. records interest expense (22,000 × .045).	dr. Interest expense 990
	cr. Interest payable 990
12/31/2 Co. records interest expense (22,990 × .045).	dr. Interest expense 1,034
	cr. Interest payable 1,034
12/31/2 Co. settles debt at maturity.	dr. Notes payable 22,000
	dr. Interest payable 2,024
	cr. Cash 24,024

6C. Pensions

Defined contribution plan Plan promises fixed annual contributions to employee's pension fund.
- This plan is more common today because it is less costly to account for and administer, and employer doesn't bear risk of future obligation. There is only one simple journal entry to record yearly pension expense: dr. Pension expense cr. Cash.

Defined benefit plan Plan promises fixed retirement benefits defined by formula.
- This plan is much less common and vanishing, even in the public sector. Unfortunately, you are still expected to know this for the exam. The rest of this chapter deals with the complex accounting for defined benefit plans.

Pension liability is reported net of plan assets, i.e., plan assets are reported in the liabilities section as an offset to pension liability.

ex. Co. has 1 employee total, who has worked 5 years—3 years vested. Current salary is $50,000. Projected to retire after 35 years of service. Projected salary at retirement is $100,000. Projected retirement period is 20 years. Co. uses formula .01 × salary × service years to calculate annual payments at retirement. Market interest rate is 6%. PVA TVMF (20, 6%) = 11.46992. PV TVMF (30, 6%) = .17411. Find Year 5 pension liability.

Liability estimates	Annual payments at retirement	PVA of annual payments in Year 35	PVA of annual payments in Year 5
Accumulated benefit obligation (ABO): Current salary, current service years.	.01 × 50,000 × 5 = 2,500	× 11.46992 = 28,674.80	× .17411 = 4,992.57 = ABO
Vested benefit obligation (VBO): Current salary, vested service years.	.01 × 50,000 × 3 = 1,500	× 11.46992 = 17,204.88	× .17411 = 2,995.54 = VBO
Projected benefit obligation (PBO): Projected salary, current service years.	.01 × 100,000 × 5 = 5,000	× 11.46992 = 57,349.60	× .17411 = 9,985.14 = PBO

- PBO is the most widely used estimate of pension liability so we'll proceed using PBO.

Changes to pension expense

1. Service and interest costs	**dr. Pension expense**	cr. Pension liability
2. Amortization of prior service cost	**dr. Pension expense**	cr. Accumulated other comprehensive income
3. *Amortization of net loss for actual return on net assets**	**dr. Pension expense**	cr. Accumulated other comprehensive income
4. *Amortization of net loss for change in PBO actuarial assumptions**	**dr. Pension expense**	cr. Accumulated other comprehensive income
5. Expected return on plan assets	dr. Plan assets	**cr. Pension expense**

- *Amortization of net loss doesn't affect pension expense until net loss exceeds a 10% corridor.

1. Service and interest costs

- **Service cost** Additional year of service.
- **Interest cost** Interest accrues on prior year PBO.

ex. Continued. PBO in Year 5 = 9,985.14. PVA TVMF (20, 6%) = 11.46992. PV TVMF (29, 6%) = .18456. Find PBO in Year 6.

Annual payments at retirement	PVA of annual payments in Year 35	PVA of annual payments in Year 6
.01 × 100,000 × 6 = 6,000	× 11.46992 = 68,819.52	× .18456 = 12,701.33

- Increase in PBO, 12,701.33 − 9,985.14 = 2,716.19, is due to service cost and interest cost.
  - Service cost component is because years of service increased by 1 year (new PV factor magnifies service cost as well).
    - .01 × 100,000 × 1 × 11.46992 × .18456 = 2,116.89
  - Interest cost component is because interest accrues on Year 5 balance.
    - 9,985.14 × .06 = 599.11 (*Differences due to TVMF rounding.*)

2. Amortization of prior service cost

- Prior service cost is accrued as a result of a plan modification (e.g. increasing the benefits formula such that pension liability increases). However, the initial recording of prior service cost has no effect on pension expense. The rationale is that the employer amended the formula and assumed more liability to benefit future operations.

Calculate prior service cost

ex. Continued. In Year 7, Co. changes formula from .01 to .025. Applies retroactively so long-time employees don't suffer vs. short-time employees.

— Year 6 pension liability if Co. doesn't change formula = $.01 \times 100,000 \times 6 \times 11.46992 \times .18456 = 12,701.33$
— Year 6 pension liability if Co. changes formula = $.025 \times 100,000 \times 6 \times 11.46992 \times .18456 = 31,753.33$
— Prior service cost = $31,753.33 - 12,701.33 = 19,052.00$

Record and amortize

- Instead of accruing pension expense all at once, we initially record a loss to OCI and then amortize AOCI and increase pension expense over time.

Co. records prior service cost.	dr. Other comprehensive income	cr. Pension liability
Co. amortizes prior service cost.	dr. Pension expense	cr. Accumulated other comprehensive income

- Most plan modifications result in a higher liability, but occasionally the company has to slash pension benefits, in which case we decrease pension expense over time.

Calculate amortization

ex. Co. calculates prior service cost of $50,000. Co. employs 6 total employees. 4 employees have 5 years until retirement and 2 employees have 2 years until retirement. Average remaining service life is 4 years = $(5 + 5 + 5 + 5 + 2 + 2) / 6$ employees.

Straight line Constant expense over average remaining service life.

— Calculate **constant** amortization expense $50,000 / 4 = 12,500$

Expected future years of service Years of service performed this year / expected future years of service.

— Calculate amortization expense   Year 1 — Year 2 = $50,000 \times 6 / 24 = 12,500$
                                               Year 3 — Year 5 = $50,000 \times 4 / 24 = 8,333$

> **Note**
>
> The following topic *Expected return vs. actual return* explains how to account for the most common decrease (5) to pension expense as well as the remaining increases (3) (4).

Expected return vs. actual return on plan assets

ex. Pension plan has $700 expected return on plan assets. Actual return is $500.

Co. decreases pension expense in the amount of expected return. The rationale is that over time gains and losses cancel each other out.	dr. Plan assets	700	cr. Pension expense	700
Co. records loss to OCI in the amount of difference between expected and actual.	dr. Other comprehensive income	200	cr. Plan assets	200

- In the above journal entries, net increase to plan assets is the $500 actual return.
- The loss is recorded to OCI. It does not reach pension expense unless/until the gap between expected return and actual return exceeds the higher of 10% of PBO or 10% of plan assets—AKA 10% corridor. Only then is the cumulative loss amortized to pension expense (over average remaining service life).
- Gain or loss on PBO due to changes in actuarial assumptions gets the same accounting based on it exceeds the higher of 10% of PBO or 10% of plan assets. Actuarial assumptions include expected retirement age, life expectancy and discount rate.

6D. Leases

Prior to the recent accounting update, companies tried to keep leases off the balance sheet because they didn't want to record the liability. Now, for all leases longer than 12 months, the lessee must report the lease on the balance sheet as both lease asset (right-of-use asset) and lease liability.

Short-term lease Lease term is 12 months or less. As mentioned above, this is the only lease that doesn't get reported on the balance sheet by the lessee.

ex. Three year lease at $1,000/month. Free first month. Bonus to lessor $3,000. Find monthly rent income (expense) for lessor (lessee). (36,000 − 1,000 + 3,000) / 36 = 1,055

- If known in advance, use variable component of rent income (expense) in calculation. If not known in advance, use in month of accrual.
- If lease renewal is probable, use both lease terms in calculation.
- **Net rental income** Gross income less property tax, depreciation and amortization of initial direct costs (appraisal, documents fee, etc).

Lease classification criteria
1. Lease transfers ownership of asset at the end of the term.
2. Lease contains a bargain purchase option—an option to buy asset in the future at a low enough price to reasonably assure exercise.
3. Lease term is for 75% of asset's remaining economic/useful life.
4. Present value of lease payments at inception is at least 90% of market value.
5. The asset has a specialized use that has no alternative use to lessor.
   - **Exception** When lease begins within last 25% of asset useful life, do not use criteria (3) and (4). Use only (1) (2) and (5).

Lease doesn't fit any criteria

To lessor, this is an operating lease.	To lessee, this is an operating lease.
• Lessor continues to record physical asset. • Lessor continues to depreciate asset over useful life.	• Lessee records right-of-use asset and payments liability. • Lessee amortizes right-of-use asset over lease term.

Lease fits one or more criteria

To lessor, this is a sales-type lease.	To lessee, this is a finance lease.
• Lessor replaces asset with lease receivable asset.	• Lessee records right-of-use asset and payments liability. • Lessee amortizes right-of-use asset over useful life.

- **Direct-financing** Lease does not qualify based on lessee payments alone, but the present value of combined lessee and third party payments equals or exceeds market value of asset. In comparison to the others, this lease classification is rare.

Lessor Operating lease

ex. On 1/1/1, lessor leases equipment for 3 years—annuity due. Equipment has fair value of $16,000, has useful life of 5 years, and has unguaranteed residual value of $2,000. Implicit rate is 6%. The lessor depreciates equipment using the straight line method. PV TVMF (3, 6%) = .83962. PVA TVMF (3, 6%) = 2.8334.

— Find lease payments to charge lessee. *Round for simplicity.*

Fair value	16,000
(PV residual value) = (2,000 × .83962) =	(1,679)
PV lease payments	14,321

Annual lease payment = 14,321 / 2.8334 = 5,054

— Prepare the journal entries.

1/1/1	dr. Cash	5,054	cr. Unearned revenue	5,054
12/31/1	dr. Unearned revenue dr. Depreciation expense	5,054 3,200	cr. Lease revenue cr. Accumulated depreciation	5,054 3,200
1/1/2	dr. Cash	5,054	cr. Unearned revenue	5,054
12/31/2	dr. Unearned revenue dr. Depreciation expense	5,054 3,200	cr. Lease revenue cr. Accumulated depreciation	5,054 3,200
1/1/3	dr. Cash	5,054	cr. Unearned revenue	5,054
12/31/3	dr. Unearned revenue dr. Depreciation expense	5,054 3,200	cr. Lease revenue cr. Acc. depreciation	5,054 3,200

Lessee Operating lease

ex. Same facts as above.

Lessee Finance lease

ex. Same facts as above except that the lease agreement explicitly transfers ownership at lease end. Additionally, the lessee uses the straight line method to amortize the right-of-use asset.

— Prepare the effective interest table. This is the same for both classifications.

Date	Payment	Interest exp — Increase to liability	Plug — Decrease to liability	Lease liability
1/1/1				14,321
1/1/1	5,054		5,054	9,267
1/1/2	5,054	556	4,498	4,769
1/1/3	5,054	285*	4,769	0

* Rounded

- **Effective interest method of amortization** Interest expense is based on (decreasing) balance of lease liability, so interest expense decreases over time. The straight-line method is not allowed unless it approximates the effective interest method.

— Prepare the journal entries. Lease liability is the same, but right-of-use asset differs. For operating lease, asset amortizes over lease term and there is only lease expense. For finance lease, asset amortizes over useful life, and there is interest expense and amortization expense.

Date								
1/1/1	dr. Right-of-use asset	14,321	cr. Lease liability	14,321	dr. Right-of-use asset	14,321	cr. Lease liability	14,321

Date								
1/1/1	dr. Lease liability	5,054	cr. Cash	5,054	dr. Lease liability	5,054	cr. Cash	5,054
12/31/1	dr. Lease expense	5,054	cr. Lease liability cr. Right-of-use asset	556 4,498	dr. Interest expense dr. Amortization exp.	556 2,864	cr. Lease liability cr. Right-of-use asset	556 2,864
1/1/2	dr. Lease liability	5,054	cr. Cash	5,054	dr. Lease liability	5,054	cr. Cash	5,054
12/31/2	dr. Lease expense	5,054	cr. Lease liability cr. Right-of-use asset	285 4,769	dr. Interest expense dr. Amortization exp.	285 2,864	cr. Lease liability cr. Right-of-use asset	285 2,864
1/1/3	dr. Lease liability	5,054	cr. Cash	5,054	dr. Lease liability	5,054	cr. Cash	5,054
12/31/3	dr. Lease expense	5,054	cr. Right-of-use asset	5,054	dr. Amortization exp.	2,864	cr. Right-of-use asset	2,864
12/31/4					dr. Amortization exp.	2,864	cr. Right-of-use asset	2,864
12/31/5					dr. Amortization exp.	2,864	cr. Right-of-use asset	2,864

- If lessee guarantees the residual value above the expected residual value, then lessee increases liability by the present value of the difference. • Disclose amount of lease payments every year for 5 future years, total remaining amount after 5 years, and total combined amount.

Lessor Sales-type

ex. On 1/1/1, lessor leases equipment for 3 years—annuity due. Equipment has $30,000 fair value, has $26,000 book value with zero accumulated depreciation (asset is new), and has 3 year useful life with no residual value. Use 6% implicit rate as above.

— Find lease payments to charge lessee.
30,000 / 2.8334 = 10,588

1/1/1	dr. Lease receivable dr. COGS	31,764 26,000	cr. Unearned interest cr. Sale cr. Equipment	1,764 30,000 26,000
1/1/1	dr. Cash	10,588	cr. Lease receivable	10,588
12/31/1	dr. Unearned interest	1,165	cr. Interest revenue	1,165
1/1/2	dr. Cash	10,588	cr. Lease receivable	10,588
12/31/2	dr. Unearned interest	599	cr. Interest revenue	599
1/1/3	dr. Cash	10,588	cr. Lease receivable	10,588

Sale-leaseback Seller-lessee sells asset (to generate cash) and then immediately leases it back. To qualify as a sale-leaseback, the leaseback must be classified as short-term lease or operating lease.
- Seller-lessee derecognizes carrying amount of asset.
- Seller-lessee records the sale and recognizes gain or loss.

Failed sale Seller-lessee attempts sale-leaseback but does not qualify because the leaseback is classified as a finance lease or sales-type lease. Seller is treated as having same rights to asset as always.
- Seller-lessee does not derecognize the asset.
- Seller-lessee accounts for cash received as a note payable (or similar financial liability).
- If seller has option to repurchase at term end, then transfer is a failed sale unless:
  - Exercise price is equal to fair value of asset at time of exercise.
  - Alternative assets are available in the market, substantially the same as transferred asset.

GAAP	IFRS
• Three lease types for lessor: operating, direct-financing and sales-type.	• Two lease types for lessor: operating and finance.

7. Deferred Taxes

Deferred tax liability (asset) Future tax sacrifice (benefit) caused by temporary differences between GAAP and tax rules. Consider the Co. that owes total income taxes of $25,000 as a direct result of Year 1 business operations. Of that, Co. must pay $20,000 in Year 2, but tax law permits Co. to pay the other $5,000 in future years. The $20,000 to be paid currently is reported in Year 1 as Income tax payable. And the $5,000 to be paid in the future is also reported in Year 1—as a deferred tax liability—because it should be reported in the same year as events that gave rise to the liability.

- Deferred tax liability = Net temporary difference × Tax rate
- Income tax payable = Taxable income × Tax rate
- Income tax expense = Income tax payable + Deferred tax liability

Temporary differences

- Straight-line vs. accelerated—Straight-line depreciation on income statement vs. accelerated depreciation on tax return.
- Accrual vs. installment method—Income recognized on income statement in year of accrual vs. recognized on tax return in year of collection.
- Accrual vs. cash method—Rent income recognized on income statement in year of accrual vs. recognized on tax return in year of collection.
- Accrual vs. cash method—Unrealized gain/loss recognized on incomes statement in year of accrual vs. recognized in year of sale, e.g., foreign currency transactions, trading securities.

ex. Tax rate is 40%. All income is collected in year of accrual. Find income tax expense for Year 1 and Year 2.

GAAP reporting	Year 1	Year 2
Revenue	120,000	120,000
Depreciation expense—Straight line	20,000	20,000
Pretax accounting income	100,000	100,000

Tax reporting	Year 1	Year 2
Revenue	120,000	120,000
Depreciation expense—Accelerated	30,000	10,000
Taxable income	90,000	110,000

— First record the balance sheet accounts, and then plug the income tax expense.

12/31/1	dr. Income tax expense	40,000	cr. Income tax payable	36,000
			cr. Deferred tax liability	4,000
12/31/2	dr. Income tax expense	40,000	cr. Income tax payable	44,000
	dr. Deferred tax liability	4,000		

Illustration

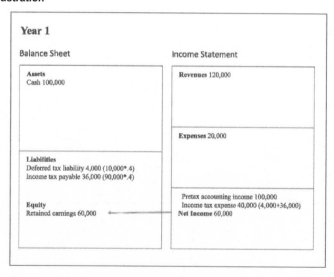
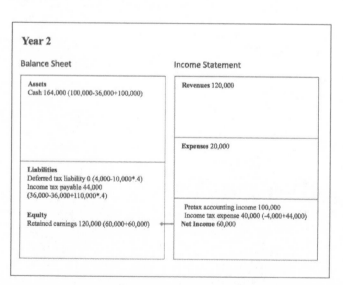

Permanent differences Activities which have different GAAP and tax reporting but which do not create deferred tax asset or deferred tax liability.

- Tax-exempt interest received from investments in state and municipal bonds AND the expenses incurred to buy the bonds.
- Tax-exempt life insurance proceeds on death of executive AND the premiums to buy the policy.
- Non-deductible expenses from law violations.

GAAP	IFRS
• Deferred tax asset is recognized in full but a valuation account is used, and the asset net of the valuation account is that which has a 50% chance of being realized.	• Deferred tax assets is recognized in part—only the part that is "probable" to be realized.

8A. Stockholders' Equity

Stockholders' equity Assets minus liabilities. AKA net assets, shareholders' equity, shareowners' equity. There are two sources of stockholders' equity: stockholder investments and corporate earnings.

Common stock rights	Preferred stock rights
<ul><li>Stockholders have voting rights (e.g., director elections).</li><li>Stockholders share in dividend distribution after preferred.</li><li>Stockholders share in liquidation after preferred and creditors.</li></ul>	<ul><li>Stockholders do not have voting rights, usually.</li><li>Stockholders have priority in dividend distribution.</li><li>Stockholders have priority in liquidation.</li></ul>

Types of preferred stock
- **Participating** Stockholders share in remainder of dividend with common stockholders.
- **Cumulative** Stockholders vest dividends even if none declared that year.
- **Convertible** Stockholders can convert preferred to common at a given ratio.
- **Redeemable** Corporation has the right to repurchase shares at given price in future.
  - **Mandatorily redeemable** Corporation must repurchase shares at given price in future. This type of stock is reported as **liability** not equity.

Stock issuance Cash received from stock issuance is net of issuing and registration expense.

Co. issues common stock.	dr. Cash dr. Issuing and registration expense	cr. Common stock cr. Paid in capital (PIC)

Stock subscription Stock-buyer commits to buy common stock in installments. Corporation does not issue until full payment. Nonpublic company may report subscription receivable as **contra equity** or **asset**. But public company must report as **contra equity**.

Co. issues subscription and receives partial payment in exchange.	dr. Cash dr. Subscription receivable	cr. Common stock subscribed **Equity** cr. PIC
Co. receives remaining payment.	dr. Cash	cr. Subscription receivable
Co. issues stock.	dr. Common stock subscribed	cr. Common stock

Treasury stock Stock the company purchased (bought back) from stockholder.
- Treasury stock is issued but not outstanding—hence it reduces weighted average common shares outstanding in Chapter 8B.

  ex.   Accounting events: 1. Co. issues 100 shares for $15 each, $10 par.
  2. Co. purchases all shares at $22 each.
  3. Co. reissues all shares at $25 each.

Cost method Treasury stock debited at cost of purchase, $2,200. With cost method, there is no positive or negative equity from treasury stock transactions until reissuance or retirement.

1.	dr. Cash	1,500	cr. Common stock cr. PIC Common stock	1,000 500
2.	dr. Treasury stock	2,200	cr. Cash	2,200
3.	dr. Cash	2,500	cr. Treasury stock cr. PIC Treasury stock	2,200 300

• Treasury stock is reported as **contra total stockholders' equity**.

Par value method Treasury stock is debited at original par of $1,000. With par value method, reissuing journal entry is similar to issuing journal entry.

dr. Cash	1,500	cr. Common stock cr. PIC Common stock	1,000 500
dr. Treasury stock dr. PIC Common stock dr. PIC Treasury stock	1,000 500 700	cr. Cash	2,200
dr. Cash	2,500	cr. Treasury stock cr. PIC Common stock	1,000 1,500

• Treasury stock is reported as **contra common stock** (or contra preferred stock if that was purchased instead). •
If purchase price is below issue price, credit PIC Treasury.

- For both methods, debit PIC Treasury if reissue is below purchase price. Debit this account down to $0 and below that debit retained earnings.
- **Retired stock** Stock the company purchased from stockholder and cancelled. Retired stock is authorized but unissued.

Dividend Allocation
1. Dividends in arrears
2. Current year preferred dividends
3. Current year common dividends
4. Participating dividends

   ex. Co. has the following shares outstanding: 2,000 cumulative participating preferred shares at $25 par with a 10% dividends rate. 3,000 common shares at $15 par. Co. owes 2 years of dividends in arrears. Co. declares $40,000 in dividends. The first $15,000 of dividend is owed to preferred stock, and the next $4,500 to common stock. All dividends in excess of $19,500 are potentially participating.

Preferred stock is cumulative, nonparticipating		Preferred stock is cumulative, participating	
Preferred stock receives $15,000 in dividends. 1. $10,000 = 2,000 \times 25 \times .10 \times 2$ 2. $5,000 = 2,000 \times 25 \times .10$	Common stock receives $25,000 in dividends. 3. $25,000 = 40,000 - 15,000$	Preferred stock receives $25,789 in dividends. 1. $10,000 = 2,000 \times 25 \times .10 \times 2$ 2. $5,000 = 2,000 \times 25 \times .10$ 4. $10,789 = 20,500 \times (50,000 / 95,000)$	Common stock receives $14,211 in dividends. 3. $4,500 = 3,000 \times 15 \times .10$ 4. $9,711 = 20,500 \times (45,000 / 95,000)$

How does accounting event impact equity?

Property dividends

Date of declaration	dr. Property dr. Retained earnings	cr. Gain on property cr. Dividends payable **Liability**	Decrease
Date of payment	dr. Dividends payable	cr. Property	

Liquidating dividends That portion of total dividends after retained earnings is depleted. In the example below, there's a $25 liquidating dividend.

Date of declaration	dr. Retained earnings 50 dr. PIC 25	cr. Dividends payable 75	Decrease

Scrip dividends Promise to pay dividends in the future. In some cases, set up as interest-bearing note payable.

Date of declaration	dr. Retained earnings	cr. Scrip dividends payable **Liability**	Decrease
Date of payment	dr. Scrip dividends payable dr. Interest expense	cr. Cash	

Stock dividends Payment of additional shares rather than cash. Stock dividend distributable is reported in equity next to common stock on balance sheet. Unlike other dividends, it is not a liability as it does not require the use of current asset, and it can be rescinded.

Date of declaration	dr. Retained earnings	cr. Stock dividend distributable **Eq** cr. PIC	No net change
Date of payment	dr. Stock dividend distributable	cr. Common stock	No net change

Stock splits No journal entry. Stock splits affect the number of shares outstanding and the par value per share, but no net change in equity.

Appropriated retained earnings That portion of total retained earnings that is not available for dividends. Includes total paid for treasury stock, using either method. Excludes dividends in arrears.

Date of appropriation	dr. Retained earnings	cr. Appropriated retained earnings **Eq**	No net change

Stock option plan The compensation plan allows employees to buy stock at predetermined price, either immediately or in the future (debit compensation expense evenly until exercise date). The fair value of option is not adjusted for changes in stock price.

ex. On 1/1/1, ABC grants president option to buy 10 shares for $20 each, $1 par once president is allowed to exercise the options on 1/1/3. The fair value of 1 option at grant date is $12.

Date of each period end	dr. Compensation expense	40	cr. PIC—Stock options **Equity**	40	Increase
Date of exercise	dr. Cash dr. PIC—Stock options	200 120	cr. Common stock cr. PIC—Common stock	10 310	Increase

- On the date of exercise, the increase to equity is equal to the cash received, $200.

Stock appreciation rights The compensation plan allows employees to receive cash equal to stock price minus predetermined price, either immediately (debit current expense) or in the future (use straight-line method to accrue expense). The fair value of option is adjusted for changes in stock price. Stock appreciation rights are classified as liability not as equity.

ex. ABC grants president 100 stock appreciation rights, can be redeemed immediately. Predetermined price is $10 per right. Stock price is $13 on 12/31/1, $12 on 12/31/2, and $16 on 12/31/3.

12/31/1	dr. Compensation expense	300	cr. SAR liability	300
12/31/2	dr. SAR liability	100	cr. Compensation expense	100
12/31/3	dr. Compensation expense	400	cr. SAR liability	400

Quasi reorganization Informal proceeding to write down overvalued assets, eliminate deficit in retained earnings.

Co. writes down overvalued assets.	dr. Retained earnings	cr. Assets	Decrease
Co. increases PIC by decreasing par.	dr. Common stock	cr. PIC	No net change
Co. eliminates retained earnings deficit.	dr. PIC	cr. Retained earnings	No net change

Corporate bankruptcy Statement of Affairs displays the current market value of the assets and classifies assets by priority.

- **Assets pledged with fully secured creditors** Assets with current value that exceed the carrying value of debt pledged against.
- **Assets pledged with partially secured creditors** Assets with current value that doesn't exceed the carrying value of debt pledged against.
- **Free assets** Assets not pledged to debt + (FV assets pledged with fully secured creditors - CV debt)

1. Creditors with priority...	2. Fully secured creditors...	3. Partially secured creditors...	4. Unsecured creditors...
...receive payment from free assets initial balance.	...receive payment in full from assets pledged with fully secured creditors.	...receive partial payment from assets pledged with partially secured creditors.	...receive payment from free assets remaining balance.

Ratios
- Book Value Per Share of Common Stock = Common Stockholders' Equity / Common Shares Outstanding at End of Period
- Rate of Return of Common Stockholders' Equity = Net Income - Current Year Preferred Dividends / Common Stockholders' Equity
- Dividend Payout = Dividends Per Share / Earnings Per Share
- Debt To Equity = Total Debt / Stockholders' Equity

GAAP	IFRS
• Proposed dividends are not required to be disclosed.	• Proposed dividends are required to be disclosed—even though dividends have not been formally approved or accrued.

8B. Earnings Per Share

Earnings per share (EPS)
1. For income from continuing operations, net of tax, report EPS on face of income statement.
2. For discontinued operations, net of tax, report EPS on face of income statement or optionally in notes to financial statements.
3. For net income, net of tax, report EPS on face of income statement.
   - There is no such thing as cash flow per share nor other comprehensive income per share.

Capital structures
- Co. with a simple capital structure—Co. with zero potentially dilutive securities—reports basic EPS figures for all three line items above.
  - Simple capital structure includes common stock, non-convertible preferred stock and non-convertible bonds payable.
- Co. with a complex capital structure—Co. with at least one potentially dilutive security—reports basic and diluted EPS for all three line items.
  - Complex capital structure includes convertible preferred stock, convertible bonds payable, stock warrants, stock options, or contingent shares.

Basic EPS = (Net Income − Current Year Preferred Stock Dividends) / Weighted Average Common Shares Outstanding

- We use net income to illustrate this formula, but you can likewise use income from continuing operations and discontinued operations.
- **Current Year Cumulative Preferred Dividends = Par Value × Dividend Rate × No. Shares**
  - Subtract current year noncumulative preferred dividends only if declared. Subtract current year cumulative preferred dividends whether or not declared. Exclude dividends in arrears.
- **Weighted Average Common Shares Outstanding (WACS)**
  - If total stockholders' equity changes during year, you must calculate the weighted average.
  - Stock dividends and splits are treated as outstanding the entire year unless stockholders have option to receive money instead of shares.

ex.			
	1/1 Co. has 75,000 shares outstanding.	75,000 × 12/12	75,000
	3/1 Co. issues 60,000 new shares.	60,000 × 10/12	50,000
	4/1 Co. issues 5% stock dividend.	Subtotal × 1.05	131,250
	10/1 Co. repurchases 10,000 shares.	(10,000 × 3/12)	(2,500)
	11/1 Co. reissues 6,000 treasury shares.	6,000 × 2/12	1,000

— WACS = 131,250 + (2,500) + 1,000 = 129,750

  - If declared after year end but before report completed, apply stock dividends and splits to the prior year.
  - For comparative income statements, apply stock dividends and splits retroactively to prior years. You don't have to restate prior year income statements, just current year comparatives.

Diluted EPS The point of diluted EPS is to calculate EPS in the most conservative way possible. We assume that company converts all potentially dilutive securities into shares of common stock. And we assume conversion happens at the beginning of the year. This increases denominator to maximum possible, and decreases EPS to minimum possible. In the event of net loss, diluted EPS is set equal to basic EPS because it is not allowed to be higher.

Diluted EPS = (Net Income + Bond Interest Expense Net Tax) / (WACS + Potential Common Stock)

- Numerator
  - If we assume that convertible preferred stock is converted to shares of common stock, then we never had preferred stock so, unlike basic EPS, we don't subtract the current year preferred dividends.
  - If we assume that convertible bond is converted to shares of common stock, then we never had bond interest and we add back bond interest expense, net of tax.
- Denominator
  - Contingent shares are treated as outstanding for the entire year if there is a time-contingency or if the contingency is based on attaining earnings levels that are already attained.

GAAP	IFRS
• Comprehensive income per share is prohibited.	• Comprehensive income per share is permitted.

9. Investments

Investor lacks significant influence Investor is presumed to lack significant influence if investor owns **less** than 20% of the voting stock.

- **Debt security** Includes bonds, notes, convertible bonds and redeemable preferred stock. Debt security has three classifications.
  - **Trading** Investor has intent to sell in the short term. Only classification that's always a current asset.
  - **Available for sale** Investor does not have intent to sell in the short term, nor does it have the ability and intent to hold until maturity.
  - **Held to maturity** Investor has ability and intent to hold until maturity. Only classification valued at amortized cost instead of fair value.

Accounting events:
1. Co. buys $900 bond with $1,000 face value.
2. Co. receives $40 interest.
3. Fair value increases $300.
4. Co. sells for $1,300.

Trading / Available for sale

1.	dr. Debt investment	1,000	cr. Discount	100
			cr. Cash	900
2.	dr. Cash	40	cr. Interest income	60
	dr. Discount	20		
3.	**dr. Fair value adj.**	**300**	**cr. Unrealized gain**	**300**
4.	**dr. Unrealized gain**	**300**	**cr. Fair value adj.**	**300**
	dr. Cash	1,300	cr. Debt investment	1,000
	dr. Discount	80	cr. Gain	380

Held to maturity

1.	dr. Debt investment	1,000	cr. Discount	100
			cr. Cash	900
2.	dr. Cash	40	cr. Interest income	60
	dr. Discount	20		
	dr. Cash	1,300	cr. Debt investment	1,000
	dr. Discount	80	cr. Gain	380

- For trading, unrealized gain/loss flows to earnings. For available for sale, unrealized gain/loss flows to other comprehensive income.

- Impairment
  - **Available for sale only** Debt security is impaired if amortized cost is above fair value.
  - **Available for sale only** Impairment loss is realized if the holder has intent to sell or it's probable the holder will be required to sell. Impairment loss is equal to amortized cost less fair value. The part of the impairment associated with investee's credit flows to earnings, and the rest (including the part associated with market decline) flows to other comprehensive income.
  - **Available for sale and held to maturity** Credit losses are recorded through an **allowance for credit loss** account, which is estimated using relevant information about past events, current conditions and reasonable forecasts. Allowance account could be estimated using discounted cash flows, for example. Make the following entry: DR Credit loss expense `Earnings` CR Allowance for credit loss.
  - **Available for sale and held to maturity** Allowance account is reassessed every year. Above entry can be reversed but not such that allowance account increases the value of the debt security.
  - **Available for sale only** Allowance account is limited by fair value (we assume the security could be sold at fair value).

- **Equity security** Includes common stock, preferred stock (except redeemable), stock warrants, call options, call rights, and put options. Investment is recorded at fair value when there is a readily determinable fair value. Otherwise, it is recorded at cost.

Accounting events:
1. Co. buys $1,000 stock.
2. Co. receives $50 dividend.
3. Fair value increases $300.
4. Co. sells for $1,300.

Fair value

1.	dr. Equity investment	1,000	cr. Cash	1,000
2.	dr. Cash	50	cr. Dividend income	50
3.	**dr. Fair value adj.**	**300**	**cr. Unrealized gain**	**300**
4.	**dr. Unrealized gain**	**300**	**cr. Fair value adj.**	**300**
	dr. Cash	1,300	cr. Equity investment	1,000
			cr. Gain	300

Cost

1.	dr. Equity investment	1,000	cr. Cash	1,000
2.	dr. Cash	50	cr. Dividend income	50
	dr. Cash	1,300	cr. Equity investment	1,000
			cr. Gain	300

- Investor is presumed to have significant influence if investor owns between 20% and 50% of the voting stock of investee.
  - But it is possible for the investor to have significant influence without 20% of voting stock.

Indicators the investor has significant influence	Indicators the investor does not have significant influence
• Investor is on the board of directors. • Investor participates in decision making • Investor has the only material voting ownership. • Investee is technologically dependent on investor. • Material intercompany transactions between investor and investee.	○ Investor is not on the board of directors. ○ Investee opposes investment. ○ Investee is in bankruptcy or subject to government restrictions.

Investor has significant influence The only reporting approach is the **equity method**. This method treats both investor and investee as one company. That means investor records income only when investee records income. The reason is that investor buys a percentage of investee total net assets, and investor net assets increase as investee net assets increase.

ex 1. Co. buys 20% of investee stock for $2,000. Book value of net assets is $10,000. Plant assets are revalued at acquisition, but plant assets FV is found to be the same as BV. Calculate goodwill.

+ Investee FV = $2,000 = Purchase price
− Investee BV = $2,000 = 10,000 × .20
− Investee—plant assets appreciation = $0

= Goodwill = $2,000 - $2,000 - $0 = $0

ex 2. Co. buys 20% of investee stock for $2,000. Book value of net assets is $7,500. Plant assets are revalued at acquisition, and plant assets FV is found to be $1,000 higher than BV. Calculate goodwill.

+ Investee FV = $2,000 = Purchase price
− Investee BV = $1,500 = 7,500 × .20
− Investee—plant assets appreciation = $200 = 1,000 × .20

= Goodwill = $2,000 - $1,500 - $200 = $300

In total, plant assets FV exceed BV by $1,000. Assume that $600 comes from inventory and $400 comes from depreciable equipment. All inventory is sold during the year. Equipment has 4 year useful life.

Accounting events:
1. On 1/1/1, Co. purchases investment for $2,000.
2. On 3/20/1, Co. receives 20% share of $500 total dividends.
3. On 12/31/1, Co. records 20% share of $1,000 net income.
4. On 1/1/2, Co. sells investment for $2,500.

1.	dr. Investment	2,000	cr. Cash		2,000
2.	dr. Cash	100	cr. Investment		100
3.	dr. Investment	200	cr. Revenue		200
4.	dr. Cash	2,500	cr. Investment cr. Gain		2,100 400

dr. Investment	2,000	cr. Cash		2,000
dr. Cash	100	cr. Investment		100
dr. Investment dr. Revenue dr. Revenue	100 120 20	cr. Revenue cr. Investment cr. Investment		200 120 20
dr. Cash	2,500	cr. Investment cr. Gain		1,960 540

• Dividends decrease investment asset but don't decrease revenue. Only net loss decreases revenue. • 120 = 600 × .20 — If inventory were written up to higher value, cost of goods sold would be higher. • 20 = 400 × .20 ÷ 4 — If machine were written up to higher value, depreciation expense would be higher during remaining useful life, and investee net income lower. • **Intercompany transactions** Profit and loss are eliminated, but receivables and payables are reported (though they need to be reported separately from other receivables and payables, and they need to be disclosed).

GAAP	IFRS
• Debt securities have three classifications: TS, AFS and HTM. • Only AFS security is recorded to OCI—OCI flows to income statement during sale. • HTM is permitted if there is intent and ability to hold to maturity. • Reversal is prohibited for impairment to debt investment. • Impairment loss on equity investment is carrying value less fair value. • All equity investors are permitted to elect fair value.	• Debt securities have two classifications: fair value through net income and HTM. • All investments may elect to record to OCI—OCI flows to retained earnings during sale. • HTM is permitted if investment passes business model test (intent) and cash flow characteristic test (serial interest payments). • Reversal is permitted for impairment to debt investment. • Impairment loss on equity investment is carrying value less recoverable amount. • Only those equity investors that are either venture capital funds, mutual funds or unit trusts are permitted to elect fair value.

10A. Fake Cash Method

Fake cash method is a natural framework for converting accrual basis to cash basis, and vice-versa. Conversions like these are also essential for preparing statements of cash flows. First, find the total increase or decrease in all related income statement, balance sheet and cash accounts—see table in Chapter 9B for related accounts. Then, within the context of a fake journal entry, debit or credit these accounts based on their normal balances.

ex. **Accrual basis to cash basis** Co. keeps books on accrual basis. On 12/31/1, accounts payable is $75,000 and inventory is $290,000. On 12/31/2, accounts payable is $50,000 and inventory of $260,000. During Year 2, Co. has cost of goods sold of $545,000. Find Year 2 cash paid to suppliers (i.e., convert from cost of goods sold, which is an accrual account, to cash paid to suppliers).

— Cost of goods sold increased by $545,000 and it is normal debit. Debit cost of goods sold.
— Accounts payable decreased by $25,000 and it is normal credit. Debit accounts payable.
— Inventory decreased by $30,000 and it is normal debit. Credit inventory.
— Cash decreased by x and it is normal debit. Credit cash.

Fake entry

(Not recorded)	dr. Cost of goods sold	545,000	
	dr. Accounts payable	25,000	
	cr. Inventory		30,000
	cr. Cash paid to suppliers		x

— Cash paid to suppliers = $540,000

ex. **Cash basis to accrual basis** Co. keeps books on cash basis. On 12/31/1, accounts receivable is $40,000, and unearned fees is $10,000. On 12/31/2, accounts receivable is $60,000, and unearned fees is $5,000. During Year 2, Co. collects $200,000 from clients. Find Year 2 revenue on accrual basis.

— Cash increased by $200,000 and it is normal debit. Debit cash.
— Accounts receivable increased by $20,000 and it is normal debit. Debit accounts receivable.
— Unearned fees decreased by $5,000 and it is normal credit. Debit unearned fees.
— Revenue increased by x and it is normal credit. Credit revenue.

Fake entry

(Not recorded)	dr. Cash received	220,000	
	dr. Accounts receivable	20,000	
	dr. Unearned fees	5,000	
	cr. Revenue		x

— Revenue on accrual basis = $225,000

10B. Statement of Cash Flows

The statement of cash flows classifies all transactions affecting cash into three categories.

1. Operating activities	Revenue Expenses Net Income

2. Investing activities	Assets
3. Financing activities	Liabilities Equity

Operating activities For exam purposes, we focus on operating activities. Both the direct method and the indirect method are permitted for the operating activities section of the statement of cash flows.

- Direct method
  - One at a time, convert each revenue (expense) account to cash received (paid). Combine to get net cash flows from operating activities.
  - Additional schedule is required for reconciliation of net income to cash from operating activities (i.e., indirect method).
- Indirect method
  - Start with net income. Reverse out income statement transactions that do not affect cash balance. Adjust for changes in operating assets and liabilities. Combine to get net cash flows from operating activities.
  - Disclose cash paid for interest and income taxes.
- For both methods, disclose non-cash investing and financing activities (at the bottom of the statement, in a separate schedule or in the notes).
- For both methods, the other sections of the statement of cash flows are the same: investing, financing and foreign currency effects.

To implement the direct method, use the fake cash method from Chapter 10A. The table below shows all related accounts.

Income statement account	Balance sheet account(s)	Cash account
Sales	Accounts receivable, unearned revenue	Cash received from customers
Interest revenue	Interest receivable	Cash received from interest
Dividends revenue	Dividends receivable	Cash received from dividends
COGS	Accounts payable, inventory	Cash paid to suppliers
Salaries and wages expense	Salaries and wages payable	Cash paid to employees
Interest expense	Interest payable, bond discount/premium	Cash paid for interest
Income tax expense	Income tax payable, deferred tax asset/liability	Cash paid for income tax

ex. Year 2 sales are $500,000. AR is $30,000 on 12/31/1 and $35,000 on 12/31/2. Find cash received from customers in Year 2.

(Not recorded)	dr. Accounts receivable	5,000	
	dr. Cash received	x	
	cr. Sales		500,000

Cash received from customers = 495,000

ex. Continued. Year 2 interest expense is $5,000. Bond discount is $3,000 on 12/31/1 and $2,800 on 12/31/2. Find cash paid for interest in Year 2.

(Not recorded)	dr. Interest expense	5,000	
	dr. Bond discount		200
	cr. Cash paid		x

Cash paid for interest = 4,800

ex. Continued. Year 2 income tax expense is $20,000. Deferred tax liability is $4,000 on 12/31/1 and $4,700 on 12/31/2. Income tax payable was $25,000 on 12/31/1 and $19,000 on 12/31/2. Find cash paid for income tax in Year 2.

(Not recorded)	dr. Income tax expense	20,000	
	dr. Income tax payable	6,000	
	cr. Deferred tax liability		700
	cr. Cash paid		x

Cash paid for income tax = 25,300

ex. Continued. Assume Year 2 depreciation expense of $5,000. Find net income and prepare cash flow statements for operating activities using both methods.

Net Income = 500,000 − 5,000 − 20,000 − 5,000 = 470,000

Direct method

Cash flows from operating activities

Cash received from customers	495,000
Cash paid for interest	(4,800)
Cash paid for income tax	(25,300)
Net cash flows from operating activities	464,900

Indirect method

Cash flows from operating activities

Net Income	470,000
Adjustments for noncash effects:	
+ Depreciation expense	5,000
+ Bad debt expense	
+ Warranty expense	
+ Losses	
− Gains	
− Equity in earnings revenue	
Changes in operating assets and liabilities:	
Accounts receivable	(5,000)
Bond discount	200
Income tax payable	(6,000)
Deferred tax liability	700
Net cash flows from operating activities	464,900

• The rule for adjustments for noncash effects: add back noncash expenses and subtract noncash revenues.

The difficulty with indirect method is figuring out whether balance sheet changes are added to or subtracted from net income. Once again, use the fake cash method. This time, use it to the change in each balance sheet account, ignoring all other variables. If fake cash account is debited, add. If fake cash is credited, subtract.

dr. Accounts receivable	5,000	cr. Cash paid	–	Subtract from net income	
dr. Cash received	+	cr. Bond discount	200	Add to net income	
dr. Income tax payable	6,000	cr. Cash paid	–	Subtract from net income	
dr. Cash received	+	cr. Deferred tax liability	700	Add to net income	

GAAP	IFRS
• Interest received is operating. • Dividends received is operating. • Interest paid is operating. • Dividends paid is financing. • Taxes paid is operating.	• Interest received is operating or investing. • Dividends received is operating or investing. • Interest paid is operating or financing. • Dividends paid is operating or financing. • Income taxes paid is operating. Other taxes attach to the category of specific item taxed.

11. Consolidated Financial Statements

Consolidated financial statements are required when investor obtains effective control over investee. Control is achieved if either of the following is true:
- Investor holds a majority of the voting shares of stock.
  - **Exceptions** The acquiree is in bankruptcy or legal reorganization or the acquiree operates in a foreign country whose government imposes financial restrictions such that there is material uncertainty regarding control.
- Investor is the principal beneficiary of a variable interest entity.
  - **Variable interest entity** Sponsor establishes an entity which intentionally cannot finance its own activities or one in which equity owners do not have power to direct significant activities.

For a group of assets to be a business, there must be an input, a substantive process to create an output, and revenue from the output. The following transactions do not constitute a business consolidation:
- Asset acquisition
  - Goodwill is not recognized in asset acquisition.
- Assets shifted between two companies that already shared common control.
  - Assets and liabilities transferred are recorded at carrying values.

Acquisition method Apply these four steps for business consolidations.

1. Identify the acquirer	Acquiree's assets, not the acquirer's, are revalued to fair value at acquisition date.
2. Determine the acquisition date	This is the measurement date, see next row. Also, after this date, acquirer recognizes net income of the acquiree.
3. Recognize and measure identifiable assets acquired, liabilities assumed, and noncontrolling interests in the acquiree	Recognizes identifiable assets, whether or not previously recognized on acquiree's books. Qualifies as identifiable asset if (1) arises from contractual right or (2) can be separately sold, transferred, etc.
4. Recognize and measure goodwill (when sum on the right is positive) OR gain from bargain purchase (when sum is negative)	+ FV of consideration transferred + FV of acquirer's previously held equity interests in acquiree + FV of noncontrolling interest − FV of net identifiable assets

- More potential gain to acquirer if consideration transferred has fair value above carrying value • Noncontrolling interest is that part of acquiree that is controlled by someone other than acquirer. Noncontrolling interest is classified as equity in the consolidated financial statements. • Acquisition-related costs are expensed, except for debt and equity issuing and registration costs. See bond issue costs in Chapter 6A. See stock issuance journal entry in Chapter 8A. • Goodwill is not amortized.

Consolidated financial statements at date of acquisition: 100% acquisition

> ex. Acquirer pays $20,000 (2,000 previously unissued shares of $5 par value common stock, now selling for $10 per share) to acquiree for all assets and liabilities. Acquiree does not dissolve (i.e., retains separate incorporation).

Accounts	Acquirer book values	Acquiree book values	Acquiree fair values
Cash	10,000	4,000	4,000
Real estate	50,000	16,000	22,000
Loan payable	20,000	5,000	7,000
Common stock	5,000	1,000	
PIC	25,000	12,000	
Retained earnings	10,000	2,000	

— (1) Acquirer records the payment to acquiree. Acquirer reports—but does not record—the new assets and liabilities. Acquirer does the reporting with the help of the worksheet below. (2) Acquirer eliminates acquiree equity, and decreases investment account. (3) Acquirer changes acquiree assets and liabilities to FV, decreases what's left of investment account, and plugs goodwill or gain on bargain purchase.

Accounts	Acquirer BS	Acquiree BS	Adjusting entries		Consolidated BS
Cash (dr)	10,000	4,000			14,000
Real estate (dr)	50,000	16,000	(3) dr. 6,000		72,000
Investment—Acquiree (dr)	(1) dr. 20,000			(2) cr. 15,000 (3) cr. 5,000	0
Goodwill (dr)			(3) dr. 1,000		1,000
Loan payable (cr)	20,000	5,000		(3) cr. 2,000	27,000
Common stock (cr)	5,000 (1) cr. 10,000	1,000	(2) dr. 1,000		15,000
PIC (cr)	25,000 (1) cr. 10,000	12,000	(2) dr. 12,000		35,000
Retained earnings (cr)	10,000	2,000	(2) dr. 2,000		10,000

Intercompany transactions At date of transaction, record intercompany transactions normally for both acquirer and acquiree. Then at consolidation, adjust all accounts to acquirer pre-sale balances. There was no transaction with unrelated party, so it's treated as if there was no transaction at all.

ex. Acquirer buys 5,000 units of inventory from unrelated third party ($4/unit). At a later date, acquirer sells 5,000 units to acquiree ($6/unit).

Acquirer books

dr. Inventory 20,000
    cr. Cash 20,000

dr. Cash 30,000
dr. COGS 20,000
    cr. Inventory 20,000
    cr. Sales 30,000

Acquiree books

dr. Inventory 30,000
    cr. Cash 30,000

— Adjust COGS, inventory, and sales to pre-sale balances of $0, $20,000, and $0. (Cash is always the same before intercompany sales as it after.)

COGS		Inventory		Sales		Consolidation adj.
20,000		20,000	20,000		30,000	dr. Sales 30,000
		30,000				cr. COGS 20,000
	Adj. 20,000		Adj. 10,000	Adj. 30,000		cr. Inventory 10,000
0		20,000			0	

GAAP	IFRS
• Control is based on majority of voting shares. • Acquirer and acquiree are not required to use same policies. • Acquirer is required to assign goodwill to noncontrolling interest based on purchase price.	• Control is based on voting shares as well as criteria like decision-making authority and appointment authority. • Acquirer and acquiree are required to use same policies. • Acquirer is not required to assign goodwill to noncontrolling interest.

12. Foreign Currency Transactions and Derivatives

FOREIGN CURRENCY TRANSACTIONS

Foreign currency transactions Transactions that create an AP or AR for US company where the payment will be received or paid in currency other than US dollars. (Contrast to Chapter 13C *Foreign Currency Translation*, which describes when an entire financial statement is converted from foreign currency to US dollars.)

	GAAP reporting	Tax reporting
Payment is not collected by year end.	Record unrealized gain/loss.	Exclude from taxable income.
Payment is collected by year end.	Record realized gain/loss.	Include in taxable income.

- When payment is not collected by year end, then there will be a temporary difference (i.e., deferred tax asset/liability) between pretax accounting income and taxable income. See Chapter 8 on deferred taxes.

GAAP reporting

ex. On 1/1, US Co. sells product to foreign company at a price of 250 euro. On same date, spot exchange rate is $0.20/€. On 2/1, US Co. received payment when spot exchange rate is $0.14/€. Transaction is collected by year end. Record transaction as gain / loss to US Co.

ex. On 12/1, US Co. purchases product from foreign company at a price of €50. On same date, spot exchange rate is €25.00/$. On 12/31, US Co. still has not sent payment and the spot exchange rate is €40.00/$. Transaction is not collected by year end. Record transaction as unrealized gain / loss to US Co.

Accounts Receivable

1/1 €250 × ($0.20 / €) = $50	
	Adj. $15
2/1 €250 × ($0.14 / €) = $35	

Accounts Payable

	12/1 €50 × ($ / €25) = $2.00
Adj. $0.75	
	12/31 €50 × ($ / €40) = $1.25

Solution

dr. Loss	15.00	
cr. Accounts receivable		15.00

Solution

dr. Accounts payable	0.75	
cr. Unrealized gain		0.75

- ○ Disclose aggregate transaction gain/loss and significant rate changes subsequent to close of reporting period.
- ○ Accounts receivable is a normal debit account, hence why the spot rates are recorded on the debit side of the T account. Accounts payable is normal credit so the spot rates are recorded on the credit side.
- ○ T account should be denominated in dollars. For the dollar to flow to the answer, you need to arrange the exchange rate so foreign currency appears in the denominator. If the exchange rate is presented euro/dollar, you need to flip the numerator and denominator. **Doing so does not change the exchange rate being expressed.** Now that the euro is in the denominator, both euro units cancel out and the dollar is the only unit remaining.

DERIVATIVES

Derivative instrument Investment in the change in value of an asset, not an investment in the asset itself. Options, futures and swaps are common examples of derivative instruments.
- Derivative instrument has all of the following characteristics:
    - ○ Derivative has little or no initial investment. In the example below, the put option cost only $150.
    - ○ Derivative contains both an underlying (value of the asset in the contract) and a notional amount (number of units specified in the contract).
    - ○ Derivative contract permits net settlement in cash or delivery in the form of an asset that's readily converted to cash. Settlement amount is similar to notional amount, except settlement amount is stated in terms of dollars.

Hedging derivatives
- **Fair value hedge** Hedge of the risk of changes in fair value of **recognized asset/liability** and **unrecognized firm commitment**.
    - ○ The gain or loss on hedge is recognized in income statement.
- **Cash flow hedge** Hedge of the risk of changes in cash flows of **recognized asset/liability** and **forecasted transaction**.
    - ○ The gain or loss on hedge is recognized in other comprehensive income.
- **Foreign currency hedge** Hedge of the risk of changes in dollar value of items that are denominated in foreign currency.
    - ○ Available for sale investment denominated in foreign currency is accounted for as a fair value hedge.
    - ○ Forecasted transaction denominated in foreign currency is accounted for as a cash flow hedge.

Put option `Fair value hedge`

ex. 1. On 1/1/1, Co. buys 100 shares of stock at $5/share. Assume stock is classified as available for sale (AFS), no fair value election.
2. On 12/31/1, stock value is $10/share.
3. On 12/31/1, Co. purchases put option for $150. The put option gives Co. the option to sell 100 shares at $10/share until 12/31/3. Co. is now protected against a decline in stock value. (Time value of hedge is $150, intrinsic value of hedge is $0).
4. On 12/31/2, stock value is $8/share. (Time value of hedge is $75, intrinsic value of hedge is $200).
5. On 12/31/3, stock value is $2/share. (Time value of hedge is $0, intrinsic value of hedge is $800).
6. On 12/31/3, Co. sells AFS stock and exercises put option.
Note: AFS security is adjusted through other comprehensive income, but gain or loss on fair value hedge is recognized in income statement.

	Journal entry	Cash (dr)	AFS stock (dr)	Put option (dr)	Hedge gain (cr)	OCI (cr)
1.	dr. AFS stock 500 cr. Cash 500	−500	500	0	0	0
2.	dr. AFS stock 500 cr. OCI 500	−500	1,000	0	0	500
3.	dr. Put option 150 cr. Cash 150	−650	1,000	150	0	500
4.	dr. Hedge loss 200 cr. AFS stock 200	−650	800	150	−200	500
	dr. Put option 200 cr. Hedge gain 200	−650	800	350	0	500
(Time value)	dr. Hedge loss 75 cr. Put option 75	−650	800	275	−75	500
5.	dr. Hedge loss 600 cr. AFS stock 600	−650	200	275	−675	500
	dr. Put option 600 cr. Hedge gain 600	−650	200	875	−75	500
(Time value)	dr. Hedge loss 75 cr. Put option 75	−650	200	800	−150	500

6.	dr. Cash 1000
	    cr. Put option 800
	    cr. AFS 200
		350	0	0	−150	500

	dr. OCI 500 cr. Hedge gain 500	350	0	0	350	0

Interest rate swap <mark>Fair value hedge</mark>

ex.   1. On 1/1/1, Co. issues $1,000,000 of 4 year, 8% fixed rate bonds.
2. On 1/1/1, Co. enters into interest rate swap. Co. to receive 8% fixed payments from XYZ, and to pay XYZ variable rates based on market interest rate. Market interest rate is currently 8%.
3. On 12/31/1, Co. makes bond payments to investors. Market interest rate is currently 5%. Co. records a loss AND increase to bonds payable liability because present value is higher using lower market rate to discount. Co. records a gain AND increase to swap contract for same amount. Let's say bonds FV is now $50,000 higher. Co. has suffered $0 net loss because of the hedge, and will record net interest expense equal to the variable market rate.

	Journal entry	Cash (dr)	Swap contract (dr)	Bonds payable (cr)	Interest expense (dr)	Holding gain (cr)
1.	dr. Cash 1,000,000 cr. Bonds payable 1,000,000	1,000,000	0	1,000,000	0	0
2.	**No entry because no purchase price for swap.**	1,000,000	0	1,000,000	0	0
3.	dr. Interest expense 80,000 cr. Cash 80,000	920,000	0	1,000,000	80,000	0

	dr. Cash 80,000
	    cr. Cash 50,000
	    cr. Interest expense 30,000
		950,000	0	1,000,000	50,000	0

	dr. Holding loss 50,000 cr. Bonds payable 50,000	950,000	0	1,050,000	50,000	-50,000
	dr. Swap contract 50,000 cr. Holding gain 50,000	950,000	50,000	1,050,000	50,000	0

Forecasted transaction denominated in foreign currency <mark>Cash flow hedge</mark>

Cash flow hedge of forecasted transaction occurs because company anticipates purchase of inventory which is listed in foreign currency. To hedge, enters into **forward exchange contract**—an agreement to exchange currencies at a specified rate on specified future date (forward rate).

ex.   On 10/1/1, US Co. contracts to purchase €50,000 in 6 months. On 10/1/1, spot rate and 4/1/2 forward rate are $.96/€ and $.97/€, respectively. On 12/1/1, spot rate and 4/1/2 forward rate are $.98/€ and $.99/€. The whole hedge is effective. Record transaction as other comprehensive gain/loss to US Co.

Accounts Receivable

10/1 €50,000 × ($.97 / €) = $48,500	
Adj. $1,000	
4/1 €50,000 × ($.99 / €) = $49,500	

Solution

dr. Accounts receivable	1,000	
cr. Other comprehensive gain		1,000

13A. Public Company Reporting

GAAP for public companies is recorded in
ASC, CFR, SEC staff guidance.

SEGMENT REPORTING

- Public companies need to disclose information about the different components of a diversified company.
- Objective of segment reporting is to assist investors who are trying to analyze and project future performance. Segment reporting should answer the following questions: What sectors of the economy does it operate in? How does each segment perform? What is the relative impact to the company? How much is from intersegment sales and how much is external?
- Segment reporting uses the management approach.
- **Operating segment** Segment for which all of the following is true:
  - Segment incurs expenses and revenues.
  - Segment is subject to review by the chief decision maker.
  - Segment is accounted for.
- Operating segment is reported if one of the following is true, based on combined amounts :
  - Segment Revenue / Total Revenue ≥ 10%
  - Segment Assets / Total Assets ≥ 10%
  - |Segment Profit (Loss)| / Larger of |Total Segments with Profit| or |Total Segments with Loss| ≥ 10%
    - Additional segments are reported in order of revenue if there are fewer than 10 reported segments or if Reported Total Revenue / Total Revenue < 75% based on consolidated amounts .
- Segment profit is reported using consolidated profit .
  - In many cases, segments can be aggregated. Reportable segments can be aggregated if similar in all criteria. Un-reportable segments can be aggregated if they are similar in a majority of criteria. Generally speaking, the criteria for aggregation deal with the nature of the products and customers.
- Company wide disclosures include all major customers, geographic areas and product revenues.
  - **Major customers and geographic areas** Revenue / Total Revenue ≥ 10% based on consolidated amounts .

Terms
  - **Combined amounts** Total amounts.
  - **Consolidated amounts** Total amounts less intersegment transactions and common costs for the benefit of several segments.

INTERIM REPORTING

- Public company reporting for periods of less than one year, e.g., monthly and quarterly reporting.
- Objective of interim reporting is to provide timely information and to inform about seasonal operations. The disadvantage of interim reporting is less reliability. As a result of the shorter reporting period, gains and losses are magnified and misleading.
- There are two methods of interim reporting: integral and discrete.
  - **Integral view** Interim periods are seen as alterable parts of the unalterable annual period, so costs may be allocated across interim periods.
  - **Discrete view** Nothing gets allocated across periods. Just like the rules for annual reporting.
- ASC does not use either method absolutely, but it generally thinks of an interim period as *"an integral part of an annual period."* As a result, expenses which clearly benefit more than one period (e.g., repairs, property tax, advertising) get allocated across several periods.
- The following items are reported integrally:
  - Cost of goods sold
    - Do not recognize temporary decline in inventory in interim report. Only recognize if decline is judged permanent.
    - Gross profit method may be used.
  - Income tax expense
    - Income Tax Expense = (Income Year To Date × Estimated Year End Tax Rate) − Income Tax Expense From Prior Quarters
- Discontinued operations is one item that is reported discretely.
  - Recognize discontinued operations in interim report in period of occurrence.

GAAP	IFRS
• Integral approach, primarily.	• Discrete approach.

13B. Partnership Accounting

Allocation of partnership income

dr. Capital account
- Distribution
- Share of loss

cr. Capital account
- Contribution
- Share of profit
- Interest on capital account
- Salary

ex. Psp. has income of $8,100 on the year. Partners A:B have 30:70 interest. Psp. makes income allocation.

	A Capital	B Capital
Capital accounts before allocation:	5,000	6,000
Psp. allocates 10% interest on capital accounts.	500	600
Psp. issues $4,000 salary to partner A.	4,000	0
Psp. allocates profit according to profit and loss percentage.	900	2,100
Capital accounts after allocation:	10,400	8,700

• Profit and loss percentage AKA partner's interest in partnership is based on written articles of copartnership. This percentage is not altered by partner contributions or distributions.

Dissolution Change in ownership event, including the admission of new partner and the retirement or death of existing partner.

ex. Partners A:B have $10,000:$7,000 capital accounts. Partners A:B have 40:60 interest. Psp admits new partner C. C contributes $3,000 for 10% interest. This contribution is greater than $20,000 × 10% = $2,000 C book value.

Bonus method	Goodwill method

C has opening capital equal to book value. Bonus is difference between contribution and book value. Bonus is allocated to old partners.
 	
dr. Cash 3,000
    cr. A Capital 400
    cr. B Capital 600
    cr. C Capital 2,000
	C has opening capital equal to $3,000 contribution. Psp. value is based on contribution, 3,000 / 10% = 30,000. Goodwill is difference between contribution and Psp. value. Goodwill is allocated to old partners.
	
	dr. Cash 3,000
	    cr. C Capital 3,000
	dr. Goodwill 10,000
	    cr. A Capital 4,000
	    cr. B Capital 6,000

ex. Partners A:B:C have $4,000:$10,000:$3,000 capital accounts. Partners A:B:C have 10:40:50 interest. Partner C receives $5,000 upon withdrawal.

Bonus method	Goodwill method

Psp. increases C capital to equal withdrawal payment, and decreases A and B to offset.
 	
dr. A Capital 400
dr. B Capital 1,600
    cr. C Capital 2,000
dr. C Capital 5,000
    cr. Cash 5,000
	Psp. increases C capital by recording $2,000 / 50% = $4,000 goodwill, and increases A and B to balance.
	
	dr. Goodwill 4,000
	    cr. A Capital 400
	    cr. B Capital 1,600
	    cr. C Capital 2,000
	dr. C Capital 5,000
	    cr. Cash 5,000

Liquidation Closing of the partnership business such that all assets sold, liabilities paid, and final distribution according to capital accounts.
- **Simple liquidation** Partnership makes distribution to partners after it sells off all assets, e.g., PP&E.
- **Installment form AKA safe payments** Partnership makes distributions before it sells off all assets. To calculate safe payments, assume that partnership discards all noncash assets for $0.

ex. Partners A:B:C have 10:40:50 interest. Psp. conducts simple liquidation:
1. Partner C repays $2,000 loan to Psp.
2. Psp. sells all PP&E for $1,000 sale ($4,000 cost).
3. Psp. pays down all liabilities.
4. Psp. distributes C's negative capital balance to other partners.
5. Psp. makes final distributions.

		Cash (dr)	Receivable: Loan to C (dr)	PP&E (dr)	Liabilities (cr)	A (cr)	B (cr)	C (cr)
	Initial Balance	12,000	2,000	4,000	1,000	4,000	10,000	3,000
1.	dr. C Capital 2,000 　　cr. Receivable 2,000	12,000	0	2,000	1,000	4,000	10,000	1,000
2.	dr. Cash 1,000 dr. A Capital 300 dr. B Capital 1,200 dr. C Capital 1,500 　　cr. PP&E 4,000	13,000	0	0	1,000	3,700	8,800	-500
3.	dr. Liabilities 1,000 　　cr. Cash 1,000	12,000	0	0	0	3,700	8,800	-500
4.	dr. A Capital 100 dr. B Capital 400 　　cr. C Capital 500	12,000	0	0	0	3,600	8,400	0
5.	dr. A Capital 3,600 dr. B Capital 8,400 　　cr. Cash 12,000	0	0	0	0	0	0	0

13C. Foreign Currency Translation

Foreign currency translation Convert financial statements denominated in foreign currency to US dollars.
- **Functional currency** The currency of cash inflows and outflows.
- **Current rate AKA spot rate** Exchange rate on balance sheet date.
- **Historical rate** Exchange rate in effect when transaction first recorded (for dividends, date declared).

Foreign currency translation gain/loss
- In the conversion process, some elements of balance sheet get multiplied by current rate, and other elements get multiplied by historical rate. This causes it to be out of balance. Foreign currency translation gain (loss) happens when balance sheet must be credited (debited) to restore balance.

There are two conversion methods:
1. Translation method AKA current rate method
    ○ Functional currency is foreign currency because operations are mostly contained within foreign country.
2. Remeasurement method
    ○ Functional currency is foreign currency but foreign economy suffers from high inflation.
    ○ Functional currency is US currency because operations are integrated within US parent company operations.

	Translation method	Remeasurement method
How to measure assets and liabilities?	Current rate	Current rate for monetary accounts Historical rate for nonmonetary accounts
How to measure stockholders' equity?	Historical rate	Historical rate
How to measure income statement accounts?	Weighted average rate for year	Weighted average rate for year
How to report translation gain/loss?	Other comprehensive income	Income from continuing operations

● Foreign currency translation gain/loss occurs because balance sheet is out of balance. ● Highly inflationary economy is defined as 100% inflation during 3 year period.

GAAP	IFRS
● Equity is measured at historical rate.	● Equity is measured at either historical rate or closing rate.

14. Governmental Accounting

GAAP for state and local governments is recorded in
GASB Codification.

- **Sources of authoritative GAAP in descending order:**
  - Category A: GASB Statements and Interpretations
  - Category B: GASB Technical Bulletins, GASB Implementation Guides and AICPA literature cleared by GASB
- **Accountability** This is the purpose of financial reporting. The public has a right to reporting information about financial condition and results of operations. Financial reporting is an important way government assumes responsibility.
- **Interperiod equity** Financial reports are used to compare current period revenue against current period expense. *Did you spend more money than you raised?* This is one of the first questions put to government because spending affects future benefits/sacrifices.
  - Financial reports are also used for comparison with legally adopted budget and compliance with finance laws and regulations.
- Financial reporting entity is comprised of the primary government and the component units.
  - **Primary government** State government or general-purpose/special-purpose local government provided it is legally separate and fiscally independent from other governments.
    - To qualify as fiscally independent, primary has to set its own budget and taxes/fees, and issue its own bonds.
  - **Component unit** Component is legally separate, and primary is either financially accountable for component or it would be misleading to omit component from financials. Generally, primary is financially accountable if component board is majority appointed (and dismissed) by primary or component is fiscally dependent on primary.
    - **Discrete presentation** Component is presented in separate column/row on financials.
    - **Blended presentation** Component funds get blended into primary funds on financials—for example, debt service fund of component flows into debt service fund of primary—provided one of the following is true:
      - Primary and component governing bodies are substantially the same.
      - Component provides services almost entirely for primary.
      - Component total debt to be paid almost entirely by primary.
- **Fund** Entity with a self-balancing set of books. Often, funds are required by law to be "separately accounted for" because restrictions are placed on their use. There are 3 fund categories.

Fund category	Accounting basis	Accounting equation
Governmental fund	Modified accrual	**Current** assets + Deferred outflows of resources − **Current** liabilities − Deferred inflows of resources = **Fund balance**
Proprietary fund	Full accrual	Assets + Deferred outflows of resources − Liabilities − Deferred inflows of resources) = **Net position**
Fiduciary fund	Full accrual	Assets + Deferred outflows of resources − Liabilities − Deferred inflows of resources) = **Net position**

- **Government-wide financial statements** consolidates governmental and proprietary funds—not fiduciary funds because the government does not own the resources therein, but only manages on behalf of others.

Government-wide	Full accrual	Assets + Deferred outflows of resources − Liabilities − Deferred inflows of resources) = **Net position**

- Statement of financial position—used for proprietary, fiduciary and government-wide—is composed of 5 elements.
  - Assets and deferred outflow of resources. Deferred outflow is the consumption of net assets to the benefit of a future period, similar to prepaid asset. Assets and deferred outflow both have a positive effect on net position.
  - Liabilities and deferred inflow of resources. Deferred inflow is the acquisition of net assets to the detriment of a future period, similar to unearned revenue. Liabilities and deferred inflow both have a negative effect on net position.
    - One of the reasons for the naming convention is so the user doesn't mistakenly combine deferred outflows with expense (or deferred inflows with revenue) in the calculation of interperiod equity.
  - Net position is just the residual of all other elements. Net position has 3 classifications.
    - **Net investment in capital assets** Capital assets at cost less accumulated depreciation less capital related debt.
    - **Restricted net position** Assets with a constraint externally imposed by creditor/grantor/other government or internally imposed by constitution/legislation.
    - **Unrestricted** All other assets.

- The term *net position* is not used for governmental funds. Instead, *fund balance* is the term and it appears on a balance sheet not on a statement of financial position (see full statement names in table below).
- Fund balance has 5 classifications listed in order of use constraints.
  - **Nonspendable** Includes supplies, inventory, and prepaid amounts.
  - **Restricted** Restraints externally imposed by creditors, grantors, other government, or internally imposed by legislation or constitution. This use restraint is legally enforceable such that the resources must be used for stipulated purpose.
  - **Committed** Restraints internally imposed by highest level of government, e.g., city council. The use restraint is not legally enforceable and these resources may be diverted to other uses, presumably in the same way it was originally committed.
  - **Assigned** Restraints internally imposed by government's intent, e.g., finance committee, program manager. These restraints can also be undone or modified.
  - **Unassigned** Remainder—may be negative if government shows deficit.
- **Modified accrual basis of accounting** Accounting basis used by governmental funds. Accounting for governmental funds is not compatible with the accrual basis. Unlike for-profits, they don't raise revenue by investing in capital or expending resources. Instead, most of the revenue is nonexchange revenue, which means it's not possible to match revenues and expenses.
  - For modified accrual, measurement focus is toward the flow of financial resources (i.e., cash and cash equivalents) and the net current financial position. The focus is to such an extreme that fixed assets and long-term debt are not recorded to the balance sheet (recall accounting formula above). These long-term items should be accounted for off-books because of their inclusion on the government-wide financial statements.
    - For accrual, the measurement focus is toward economic resources (i.e., long-term items included) and the net financial position.
  - For modified accrual, revenue recognition occurs in the period that revenue is measurable and available. *Available* means the revenue is received in time to pay current year expense and it includes collections up to 60 days after year end.
    - For accrual, revenue recognition occurs in the period that revenue is measurable and earned.
  - For modified accrual, expense recognition is much different. First, the term in governmental fund accounting is *expenditures* not *expense*, but it means essentially the same thing (expenditures is a temporary account that decreases financial resources). In substance, expenditure recognition differs in the following ways:
    - Capital-related expenditure is recorded to expenditure account not to asset account. Balance sheet lacks a fixed asset account (AKA property, plant and equipment).
    - Interest expenditure on general long-term debt (term refers to debt held by governmental funds) is not recorded until due date.
      - When debt is held by proprietary funds, which always operate on accrual basis, interest expense is called specific long-term debt and it's accrued normally.
    - Supplies and prepaids may be recorded to expenditures at time of use (accrual) or at time cash is paid (not accrual).

Comprehensive Annual Financial Report (CAFR) Most state and local governments produce a Comprehensive Annual Financial Report. This report contains an introduction section, financial section and statistical section.
- **Introduction section** Includes table of contents, transmittal letter and general information.
- **Financial section** Includes auditor's report, **General Purpose Financial Statements**, and other supplementary information (not required supplementary information).
- **Statistical section** Includes trends, revenue sources, debt ratios, demographic information and economic information.

General Purpose Financial Statements This is the minimum requirement for external reporting.
1. Management's discussion and analysis (MD&A)
   - MD&A is used to assess financial condition, change from last year, and to compare budget amounts to actual amounts.
   - MD&A is required supplementary information.
2. Basic financial statements

Government-wide financial statements	<ul><li>S. Net Position</li><li>S. Activities</li></ul>		
Fund financial statements	Governmental funds	Proprietary funds	Fiduciary funds
	<ul><li>Balance Sheet</li><li>S. Revenues, Expenditures, Changes in Fund Balances</li></ul>	<ul><li>S. Net Position</li><li>S. Revenues, Expenses, Changes in Fund Net Position</li><li>S. Cash Flows</li></ul>	<ul><li>S. Fiduciary Net Position</li><li>S. Changes in Fiduciary Net Position</li></ul>
Notes to financial statements	• Summary of significant accounting positions		

● Fiduciary funds are excluded from government-wide financial statements. ● Government-wide financials demonstrate operational accountability, while fund financials demonstrate fiscal accountability. ● Special-purpose government engaged in a single governmental activity may combine government-wide and fund statements.

3. Required supplementary information other than MD&A
   - Ten-Year Schedules of Selected Information related to pension plans.
   - Budgetary Comparison Schedules.
   - Information about Infrastructure Assets using modified approach to infrastructure.

Governmental funds

1. **General fund** Remainder fund. Government has only one general fund. It is always a major fund, whereas other funds below may not be. And it is the only fund that can have a positive unassigned balance.
2. **Special revenue fund** Funds from a specific source and limited to a specific function not debt-service nor capital projects, e.g., fuel tax limited for roadways.
3. **Debt service fund** Funds used for payment of debt principal and interest.
4. **Capital projects fund** Funds used for capital outlays, e.g., proceeds from bond issue for building.
5. **Permanent fund** Funds from endowment used for government programs. Fund is not allowed to spend in private sector, or it becomes a private purpose trust fund. Fund is limited to spending earnings. It is not allowed to spend principal or it becomes a special revenue fund.

   - General fund and special revenue fund are the only funds to use budgetary accounting and encumbrance accounting. ● Fund financial statements must show reconciliation between governmental fund financial statements and governmental activities section of government-wide financial statements. Governmental activities section of government-wide = Governmental funds + Capital assets + *Internal service fund**.

Proprietary funds

6. **Internal service fund** Funds provide goods and services at cost to other parts of government, e.g., print shop, motor pool. *Internal service fund** is generally reported in governmental activities column in government-wide S. Net Position. However, if the primary customers are enterprise funds, then internal service fund is reported in the business-type activities column.
7. **Enterprise fund** Funds provide goods and services to external users for a fee, e.g., water utility, airport, university, lottery. Enterprise fund is the only fund to have a profit motive similar to private sector GAAP. This fund is reported in business-type activities column in government-wide S. Net Position.

   - S. Cash Flows pursuant to ~~FASB~~ GASB
     - Statement has four sections: operating, investing, noncapital financing, capital financing.
     - Statement uses direct method. There is no option to use indirect method. Additionally, there is a reconciliation from ~~net income~~ operating income to net cash flow from operating activities.
     - Interest received is ~~operating~~ investing.
     - Purchase of capital asset provided by financing activity is ~~investing~~ capital financing.

Fiduciary funds

8. **Custodial fund** Fiduciary activities that are not required to be reported in the other fund types. This is a new fund type and, unlike its predecessor, it has the same elements as the other fiduciary funds and has the same reporting requirements: S. Fiduciary Net Position and S. Changes in Fiduciary Net Position.
9. **Pension and other employee benefit trust funds** Funds held in trust for employee retirement.
10. **Investment trust fund** Funds in investment pool that reflect other government's share of pool.
11. **Private-purpose trust fund** Funds, limited to earnings, held to benefit individuals or entities other than government.

GOVERNMENTAL ACCOUNTING—OTHER ITEMS

Nonexchange revenue Transactions in which government receives value without directly giving equal value in exchange. There are four categories.

Derived tax revenue Taxes on transactions.	Imposed nonexchange transactions Taxes and other assessments not on transactions.	Government-mandated nonexchange transactions Government must accept money and spends for specific purpose.	Voluntary nonexchange transactions Government may accept money and, if accepted, spends for specific purpose.
ex. Sales tax, Income tax, Fuel tax, Unemployment tax.	ex. Property tax, Estate tax, Special assessment, Fine.	ex. States mandated to perform federal program.	ex. Private donations to government for education.

Intangible assets For internally generated intangibles to be capitalized, payments are expensed until demonstration of feasibility and intention to/ability to complete, at which point payments are capitalized.

Software For internally generated software, only activities performed in the application development stage are capitalized. These activities include design, software configuration, coding, installation and testing.

Service concession arrangements Public-private partnership in which private operator agrees to build or operate government facility in exchange for a percentage of the fees collected from third party users, e.g., the public. Usually the operator fronts a payment to the government and the government sets it up as a liability—credit deferred inflow—to be earned over time.

Subsequent events Events that occur after the S. Net Position date but before the financial statements are issued.
- Recognize in financial statements if conditions already existed at S. Net Position date, e.g., customer bankruptcy affects bad debt expense.
- Disclose in notes if condition did not exist at S. Net Position date.

Governmental colleges and universities
- Primary government reports colleges and universities as component units on the government wide financial statements.
- Colleges and universities use the same set of financials statements as proprietary funds.

ACCOUNTING FOR GOVERNMENTAL FUNDS

General Fund

1. Gov. adopts a budget.
   - Budgetary accounting is unique to governmental funds.
   - **Appropriations** Estimated expenditures.

dr. Estimated revenues	50,000	cr. Appropriations cr. Estimated other financing uses cr. Budgetary fund balance	40,000 8,000 2,000

2. Gov. transfers to a debt service fund.

dr. Other financing uses—operating transfer to debt service fund	10,000	cr. Cash	10,000

3. Gov. makes property tax assessments.
   - Unlike revenue, a receivable is recognized without regard to availability of funds. For derived taxes, receivable is recognized when the underlying exchange takes place. For imposed taxes, receivable is recognized when there is an enforceable legal claim (as happens on the assessment date).
   - Procedurally, revenue is also recognized on this date without regard to availability of funds. But at year end, there is an offsetting debit for that portion that is not expected to be available to pay this year's expenses.

dr. Property taxes receivable	40,000	cr. Estimated uncollectible taxes cr. Revenues	4,000 36,000

4. Gov. earns revenue from fines, licenses and permits.

dr. Cash	4,000	cr. Revenues	4,000

5. Gov. expects to collect revenue from state after year end but in time to pay current year expenditures.

dr. State sales tax receivable	8,000	cr. Revenues	8,000

6. Gov. has expenditures for salaries, utilities, and rent.

dr. Expenditures	35,000	cr. Vouchers payable	35,000

7. Gov. orders stop sign for $500 and radar gun for $750.
   - For modified accrual, transactions that are executory in nature (e.g. order, purchase order, signed contract) are recognized accounting events.
   - Budgetary fund balance committed (or assigned, if not imposed by highest level of government) is always equal and opposite to encumbrances.

dr. Encumbrances dr. Encumbrances	500 750	cr. Budgetary fund balance committed cr. Budgetary fund balance committed	500 750

8. Gov. receives stop sign, actual cost $400.

dr. Budgetary fund balance committed dr. Expenditures	500 400	cr. Encumbrances cr. Vouchers payable	500 400

9. Gov. pays expenditures for salaries, utilities and rent.

dr. Vouchers payable	35,000	cr. Cash	35,000

10. Gov. purchases $150 in supplies. By year end, supplies inventory has unused balance of $60.
- This is the purchases method, but consumption method is also allowed by modified accrual.

dr. Supplies expenditure	150	cr. Cash	150
dr. Supplies inventory	60	cr. Fund balance—nonspendable	60

11. By year end, Gov. has collected $37,000 in property taxes. Gov. expects to receive another $1,000 from property taxes receivable, but not in time to pay this year's expenses.

dr. Revenues	1,000	cr. Deferred revenues—property taxes	1,000
dr. Cash	37,000	cr. Property taxes receivable	37,000
dr. Estimated uncollectible taxes	2,000	cr. Revenues	2,000

12. Gov. closes the budget.

dr. Appropriations	40,000	cr. Estimated revenues	50,000
dr. Estimated other financing uses	8,000		
dr. Budgetary fund balance	2,000		

13. Gov. closes temporary accounts to fund balance account.

dr. Revenues	49,000	cr. Expenditures	35,550
		cr. Other financing uses	10,000
		cr. Fund balance—unassigned	3,450

14. Gov. closes out encumbrances not received and makes adjustment to balance sheet accounts.

dr. Budgetary fund balance committed	750	cr. Encumbrances	750
dr. Fund balance—unassigned	750	cr. Fund balance—committed	750

Debt Service Fund

1. General fund transaction #2

dr. Cash	10,000	cr. Other financing sources—operating transfer from general fund	10,000

2. Gov. records interest.
   - *Expenditures—interest* is reported on the fund financial statement, while *Interest expense* is reported on the government wide financial statement.

dr. Expenditures—interest	10,000	cr. Interest payable	10,000

3. Gov. pays interest.
   - Under modified accrual, interest is accrued when legally due, not at period end.

dr. Interest payable	10,000	cr. Cash	10,000

Capital Projects Fund

1. Gov. issues bonds to finance project.
   - *Other financing sources—bond proceeds* is reported on the fund financial statement, while *Bonds payable* is reported on the government wide financial statement.

dr. Cash	100,000	cr. Other financing sources—bond proceeds	100,000

2. Gov. accepts bid from builder.

dr. Encumbrances	90,000	cr. Budgetary fund balance committed	90,000

3. Gov. has expenditures for work in progress.
   - *Contracts payable—retained* is a liability account. Government withholds portion of money from builder until final inspection and approval.

dr. Budgetary fund balance committed	20,000	cr. Encumbrances	20,000
dr. Expenditures	20,000	cr. Cash	19,000
		cr. Contracts payable—retained	1,000

15. Not-for-Profit Accounting

GAAP for not-for-profits is recorded in
ASC.

For general private sector nonprofit organizations, financial statements consist of S. Financial Position, S. Activities, S. Cash Flows, and notes to the financial statements. S. Functional Expenses may or may not be prepared. Financial statements are prepared on the accrual basis of accounting.

S. Financial Position
- Includes sections for assets, liabilities, and net assets.
- Assets are classified in order of liquidity, not as current and noncurrent.
- Net assets are classified in two ways.
    1. **Net assets without donor restrictions** No donor-imposed restrictions. Please note that donation is unrestricted if governing board sets restrictions on revenue. Donation is likewise unrestricted if donor mandates donation must be used in current year.
    2. **Net assets with donor restrictions** These restrictions may be temporary or permanent in nature.
        - **Temporary restriction** Donor imposes time or purpose restrictions.
        - **Permanent restriction** Donor imposes restriction in perpetuity, e.g., investment principal belonging to a regular endowment.

S. Activities

+ Changes in net assets without donor restrictions

    Components
    Contribution revenue
    Exchange revenue
    Net gains on investments
    Net assets released from restrictions
    (Expenses and losses)

+ Changes in net assets with donor restrictions

    Components
    Contribution revenue
    Investment income from endowment
    (Net assets released from restrictions)

= Changes in total net assets
+ Beginning net assets

= Ending net assets

- Revenues
    - **Contribution revenue** Money received for which nonprofit gives nothing in return. Contribution revenue can be found in both sections of S. Activities because contributions may come with or without donor restrictions.
    - **Exchange revenue** Money received for which nonprofit gives something back of equal value, e.g. fees, dues, charges for services. Exchange revenue must come without donor restrictions.
- Expenses and losses
    - Expenses must be reported by function and by nature in the same location. This can be done right here on the face of the S. Activities, or in the notes to the financial statements or optionally as a separate statement, S. Functional Expenses.
    - Functional expense can be a program service or a supporting service. Program service refers to expenditure for a distinct purpose or mission. Supporting service refers to expenditure for management or fundraising.
    - Natural expense includes rent, utilities, interest, etc. in other words the default expenses we're used to seeing on for-profit income statements.
- Net assets released from restrictions
    - Nonprofit cannot directly expense net assets with donor restrictions.
    - Assets that have satisfied all donor restrictions are said to have been released from restrictions. From then on, these assets can be expensed.
    - The line item *Net assets released from restrictions* appears twice in S. Activities because there is a decrease to net assets with donor restrictions and an increase to net assets without restrictions.

ex.   Accounting events: 1. On 3/1, nonprofit receives $750 of restricted contribution revenue.
                                      2. On 6/15, nonprofit satisfies the restriction and expenses.

1.	dr. Cash	750	cr. Contribution revenue—donor-restricted	750
2.	dr. Contribution revenue—donor-restricted dr. Program expense	750 750	cr. Contribution revenue—without donor restriction cr. Accounts payable	750 750

S. Cash Flows
- Cash flow from operating activities includes most contribution and exchange revenue. There are two carve outs that are treated as cash flow from financing activities: endowments and long-term restrictions on capital assets.

OTHER ITEMS AND TRANSACTIONS

- **Endowments**
  - **Permanent endowment AKA regular endowment** Contributed funds such that the principal has a permanent donor restriction.
  - **Term endowment** Contributed funds such that the principal has a temporary donor restriction.
  - **Quasi-endowment** Governing board internally restricts funds for investment such that the principal cannot be spent.
    - Principal has internal restriction, but does not have a donor restriction.
  - **Board-designated endowment** Governing board internally designates funds for investment, but principal is allowed to be spent.
    - Principal has internal designation, but does not have a donor restriction.
- **Pledge** Nonprofit recognizes revenue on pledge date. And a pledge receivable is likewise set up on pledge date, with an allowance for estimated uncollectible pledges.
  - This assumes no condition has been placed on the pledge. See *conditional contribution* below.
  - Revenue recognition has nothing to do with date of receipt.
- **Donated service** Nonprofit recognizes a revenue at fair value, provided service meets one of the following:
  - Service enhances a non-financial asset, e.g., builder builds for a nonprofit. Nonprofit debits asset and credits revenue.
  - Service is a specialized skill, service is normally purchased, and it is performed by someone who actually possesses that skill. In this case, nonprofit debits expense and credits revenue. This entry affects the ratio of program expenses to total expenses AKA program ratio, which measures how responsibly nonprofits spend their money.
- **Donation over multiple periods** Nonprofit recognizes revenue at net present value of total donation. All revenue is recognized upfront.
  - Some of the revenue has time restrictions (the portion that's expected in future periods). When a future year donation is received, net assets in that amount are released from restriction.
  - Net present value is recalculated at year end and the change in value is credited to, or debited against, restricted revenue.
- **Gains and losses on investment** Nonprofit recognizes unrealized gains or losses as a result of changes in fair value.
  - There are no sub-classes of securities like trading, available for sale or held to maturity. Instead, nonprofit reports all securities—even debt securities—at fair value.
- **Agent transactions** Nonprofit-agent may or may not recognize revenue depending on whether it has variance power.
  - Agent is a large nonprofit who raises money on behalf of smaller nonprofits. Most well known agent is United Way.
  - Variance power is the ability to redirect contribution without donor's approval.

ex.   Accounting events: 1. On 4/1, agent receives $500 donation.
                              2. On 4/5, agent disburses the whole amount to nonprofit.

Agent does not have variance power.
(Donor selects nonprofit directly.)

1.	dr. Cash	500	cr. Liability	500
2.	dr. Liability	500	cr. Cash	500

Agent has variance power to select nonprofit or agent is financially related to donor.

dr. Cash	500	cr. Contribution revenue	500
dr. Contribution expense	500	cr. Cash	500

- **Conditional contribution** Nonprofit does not recognize revenue. Conditional contribution is not revenue and if donor actually makes the deposit, it is a liability until revenue is recognized or money is returned.
  - To recognize revenue, the condition has to substantially met or the possibility becomes remote that condition will not be met.
  - Please note that a condition on money is different from a restriction on money. A restriction on money is still revenue.
- **Deferred revenue** Nonprofit recognizes a liability. Despite its name, deferred revenue is not a revenue. It occurs when nonprofit receives a deposit for work that it will perform in the future.

Made in the USA
Columbia, SC
27 October 2020